Sermons preached in the Church of our Saviour, Jenkintown, Pa.

Richard Francis Colton d. 1880

R. Francis Colton

SERMONS

PREACHED IN THE

CHURCH OF OUR SAVIOUR,

JENKINTOWN, PA.

BY THE LATE RECTOR,

Rev. R. FRANCIS COLTON,

PROFESSOR OF HEBREW IN THE PROT. EPISCOPAL DIVINITY SCHOOL, WEST PHILADELPHIA

PHILADELPHIA:

EPISCOPAL BOOK STORE.

1224 CHESTNUT STREET.

CONTENTS.

———

iv   CONTENTS.

INTRODUCTION.

THE proper disposal of the MSS. which constitute these sermons, has been a subject of anxious thought. They were written, and preached for the most part in Jenkintown, Pa., where, nearly twelve years ago, the REV. RICHARD FRANCIS COLTON, then in the first ardor of youth, came to minister as Rector in the Church of Our Saviour.

Combining with his parish duties the Professorship of Hebrew in the Divinity School at West Philadelphia, he lived his quiet student life away from the city, adding day by day to the vast intellectual store that made him emphatically "a scholar, and a ripe and good one."

He had been ordained to the Diaconate in the Church of the Atonement in Philadelphia, on the 21st of February, 1866, and officiated in that church until June, 1867, as Assistant to the Rev. Benjamin Watson, D. D.

When, after a few hours' illness, on the 28th of July, 1880, it was known that he had been taken away, all in his parish felt it to be a personal loss. It seemed impossible to associate the idea of death with that bright, genial nature that carried an atmosphere of health wherever he went.

To those of his congregation who knew him best, these pages will need no explanation. They will reiterate with new force, as of a voice from the dead, their message of earnest appeal to duty, and their keen appreciation of the sorrows and the struggles that he had so often shared in sympathy.

That he shrank from the publication of any of his sermons during his life is well known ; but now that he can speak only through them, they are felt to be too sacred, too important a trust to be withheld.

They are printed as he left them, without revision, even when it seems obvious that his own hand would have made changes. They are the best memorial of a noble, manly nature, that was child-like in tenderness for suffering, and stern to severity in hatred of folly and shams.

M. E. S.

PHILADELPHIA, *Feb.* 1, 1882.

SERMONS.

I.

THE INSPIRATION OF SCRIPTURE.

"Ye see how large a letter I have written unto you with mine own hand."—GAL. vi. 11.

THE literal meaning of St. Paul's words in this passage is: "Ye see in what large letters I have written unto you with mine own hand." The passage has received several different interpretations. It has been supposed by Chrysostom and others that the words "point to the rude and ill-formed characters in which the letter to the Galatians was written, as though he gloried in his imperfect knowledge of Greek." But the word used means "how large," and "how large" only. According to others, we have here an allusion to that thorn in the flesh to which he elsewhere refers, and which was, apparently, in part, at least, an infirmity of vision. The explanation of the way in which he came thus to speak then, will harmonize perfectly with the tone that prevails throughout this Epistle —the deep personal affection which leads St. Paul with almost passionate yearning, to plead with his spiritual children to give up the delusions into which false Jewish teachers were leading them; — which finds vent again and again, in words the most exquisitely tender and pathetic:

1

The expression here employed summons up the picture of the care-worn Apostle, mourning over his converts in their abandonment of the great spiritual truths he had so patiently preached to them, and their too-ready relapse into bondage to *the weak and beggarly elements of the world, to work unrighteousness.* Unwilling to lose any possible advantage in his earnest and sorrowful pleadings with them — unwilling to forego the influence which might perhaps be exerted upon them by a more vivid recollection of his personal sacrifices for them, or of the love which had once made them willing to pluck out their own eyes if they might only relieve his, and so lighten a little the burden resting on his overladen shoulders,—he rejects the aid of the scribe, who, as we learn from the ending of other letters, ordinarily wrote at his dictation, and, painfully struggling with his dimmed eyesight, writes out himself in full, in such large letters as alone he could plainly discern, the utterance of his grieved and wounded heart, of his holy indignation at those who had dared to undermine by false teaching the foundations he had so toilsomely laid, of his burning logic, consuming the hay and stubble which they had tried to put in the place of that one foundation, Jesus Christ the Lord.

Does not that simple word bring before you with marvellous clearness, not only the personal character of the great Apostle, but the spirit in which he labored—the passionate self-devotion with which he gave himself up to his work? Do you not feel as though the eighteen centuries that part us were done away, and you stood face to face with that sublime hero of the faith? Do not the burning words take on a fresh fire and meaning, as though from some old mosaic the dust of ages were cleared away, and its tints shone out as clear as when Pompeii was buried in the ashes of Vesuvius.

I am led by the occurrence in the Epistle for the day of these words of St. Paul, to think of the general subject which they suggest — I mean the preservation in the Scriptures of the personal characteristics of the holy men of old whom the Holy Ghost moved from time to time to write them, and so of Inspiration in general. The whole question of the Inspiration of the Bible is one regarding which there prevail mistakes which are dangerous in both directions. On the one hand you find ardent believers who feel that the Bible is nothing worth unless they can hold that every word of it is the absolute and immediate utterance of the Holy Ghost; and this in such a sense that the inspired writer was no more than the passive instrument in the hand of the Spirit — no more than a pen moved and guided by God. Seeing how much in Scripture is impossible to reconcile with this, many, on the other hand, attach to the variations of style,—to the large class of passages like the text,—an importance so excessive, that they can nowhere discern anything more than the utterances of men who enjoyed, indeed, a peculiarly close connection with God, but who nevertheless, spoke in a manner, and delivered truths that need no explanation further than their possession of large spiritual experience and deep spiritual insight.

Either view, pushed to such an extreme, is guilty of overlooking facts which lie, as it were, upon the surface of the subject. And, inasmuch as none should be so eager to have and to hold the exact truth on this matter as those who wish to reverence God's Revelation as it deserves, none should be readier to examine the facts before us carefully and with an unbiased mind. Let us remember how the truth of Christ's incarnation has been overlooked by the same spirit which would be wise beyond what is written; let us recall the lamentable consequences of that superstitious spirit which is not content with the simplicity that marks God's works, but which runs to seed in the invention of miracles and visions. And wise in the knowledge that God is, above all, reasonable in his demands upon our faith, and gives us the why and the wherefore for even the mysteriousness of the mysteries he displays, let us approach this subject with the honest desire to see what the record itself should reasonably lead us to believe.

And in the first place, does any portion of any of the numerous books, the collection of which forms what we call the Bible—the Book—does any part of it profess to be an immediate revelation from God? In the book of Esther the name of God does not occur. The historical books, as to their historical portion, make no such claim. The Gospels do not pretend to the character of immediate revelations. What are we to conclude from this? That they are only compilations, written by men with no greater claims upon our belief than any ordinary annalist, or eye witness of the facts related? If such were the necessary conclusion—if there were no reasons to lead us to any belief, what then? It would be a great shock to our ordinary beliefs certainly; it would shatter at a blow much of what is endeared to us by a thousand hallowed associations; it would make needful a great change in the manner in which we ordinarily make use of the Bible; but still, supposing the Scriptures to make no claims of this kind,—supposing that by carefully searching we could find no ground for our customary belief except the tradition of a few thousands of years, how could we dare to father upon God immediate responsibility for that which we should have no reason for attributing directly to Him? Would it be honoring or dishonoring to God? Would it be pious or impious? Ask yourself that question, and you will have prepared yourself to go on by honestly answering: "No. If this belief is only a vain human tradition—if it has no real ground, I must give it up— I have no right to ascribe the Bible to God."

I have put this so strongly because I am sure it is the only way in which we can make firm the foundation of our faith. St. Paul himself will be the first to bid you be ready to give a reason for the faith that is in you. So only can you stand firm.

I have said that certain books and certain parts of books make no express claim to being inspired. Do we find anywhere a claim of this kind? Unquestionably we do, and a claim quite unmistakable: Constantly is this the case throughout the four later books of Moses, and in the Prophets, so far as the Old Testament is concerned. "Thus saith the Lord" is the perpetually recurring introduction to the sublime messages of the Hebrew seers. Even granting that the Gospels do not profess to be inspired, they still remain, on the lowest view, narratives of the life and death of Christ, written at all events by men who were eye-witnesses (as St. Matthew and St. John), or men having access to all sources of knowledge of the facts they relate. And what do they say of Christ's way of speaking about the Old Testament? We know that He spoke of all the three divisions into which the Jews distributed their sacred books—the Law, the Psalms and the Prophets; that the

Jews had the same books which we have now, and that
Christ quotes and refers to them as being the Word of God.
There is no more hesitation in His manner of using them—
no more doubt that He was employing the words of infallible truth—than we have to-day. Their prophecies concerning himself He makes use of as being Divine revelations,
which He had left the bosom of the Father to fulfil. Merely casual expressions, as we might think, such as Jehovah's
calling himself the God of Abraham, Isaac and Jacob,
Christ uses to prove the (then) dimly revealed doctrine of
immortality, as though every word of the Old Testament
were pregnant with spiritual truth. He exhorts those who
were cautiously hesitating about the acknowledgment of
His claims, to search the Scriptures, approves their belief
that in them they had eternal life, and asserts in a way
which can only mean that they spoke the truth, that they
are they which testified of Him.

I address, of course, only those who believe in the
divinity of Christ, which would stand firm were the inspiration of the Gospels denied. Once grant the Gospels are
honest accounts of Christ, and you have a character which
is its own sufficient evidence; you regard His words as
strong enough evidence of the statements He makes.
Standing on this impregnable foundation, look behind you
and before you—upon the Old Testament, and upon the
Apostolic writings of the New Testament. You find Him
distinctly promising that his Apostles should have the
Holy Ghost to guide them into all truth, bidding them not
to think beforehand what they should say when summoned
before their enemies, because the Holy Ghost should teach
them what to say, " For it is not ye that speak, but the
spirit of your Father that speaketh in you." A more un-

limited promise, so far as the *fulness* of inspiration is concerned, it would be hard to conceive. I ask nothing further than the acknowledgment of the honesty of the report given of His words by St. John, His most intimate and beloved companion; and we must look upon the Apostles as men to whom it was promised that the Holy Ghost should take of the things of Christ and show them unto them. But in the last hours of our Saviour's life, He prayed not for them only who then slumbered near Him, but for those as well who should afterwards believe on Him. If we believe as Christians in the divinity of Christ, which I here make no attempt to prove, such thoughts must continually have been present to His mind; and indeed His words afford frequent glimpses of both His anticipations for the future of His Church, and His immovable confidence that those anticipations would be fulfilled. Does not the supposition amount to a certainty, then, that the Holy Ghost, which was promised to teach the Apostles what to say and how to say it before courts and synagogues, would not desert them when they came to set down in writing, for various exigencies, the truths of Christ's kingdom—that this divine illumination would not be confined to fleeting words uttered by the lips, but would extend likewise, and particularly, to the *writings* which were to hand down those truths in permanent shape to generations yet unborn? And if, as Christ always assumes, the Holy Ghost spake of old by Prophet and Psalmist, so that their words could be unhesitatingly applied to the proof and illustration of divine truth, if the human mind *could* serve as the mouthpiece of the divine mind in days of partial light, much more, if possible, was it to be expected that under the dispensation of the Spirit that mysterious influence should be permanent and distinct. But turn from suppositions and probabilities: ask the Apostles of what they were conscious in the depths of their own souls. Does St. Paul impress you as a weak-minded, visionary character, easily led astray by flattering fancies, or as a clear-minded, hard-headed, thoroughly honest man, who never feared to do or say anything which he believed to be right, and yet who could speak when he was persuaded he was wrong, even to the length of sacrificing his life to the propagation of the Gospel which at first he had persecuted? What did he think of the way in which he had acquired the truth he so fearlessly proclaimed? In this very epistle, wrung from his very heart's blood, and whose words were, as I have said, painfully traced in those great letters by one whose bodily eyes were dim, but whose spiritual vision was certainly not overcast—in this same epistle to the Galatians he says, "I neither received it of man, neither was I taught it but by the revelation of Jesus Christ." Again: "The things that are freely given unto us of God"; "We speak, not in the words which man's wisdom teacheth, but which the Holy Ghost teacheth." Again and again in St. Paul's epistles, in those of St. Peter and of St. John, particularly in the Revelation, is this inspiration referred to, as something not so much claimed as universally acknowledged.

At last the canon of Scripture is closed. For a time the books of the New Testament are not collected into a single volume. Do we find those who knew, or those who immediately followed the Apostles, ignorant of their writings, or of the Gospels of St. Luke or St. Mark, or quoting as New Testament Scripture anything now lost,

THE INSPIRATION OF SCRIPTURE.

or acknowledged as uninspired by the Church of after ages? Not at all. The very same writings which now make up the New Testament, though, as I have said, not yet collected into one volume, are their New Testament as they are ours. Though peculiar circumstances seem to have hindered the spread of St. James and St. Peter's second Epistles, the Epistle to the Hebrews, and the Apocalypse, yet we find them early quoted as Scripture; and at the very time when what are called the books of the Apocrypha, or forged New Testament, were universally rejected, these are only doubted in some quarters and are finally received with entire unanimity. The church was very cautious in admitting books to the canon; but the existence of doubts, followed by investigation and consequent abandonment of those doubts, constitutes only a stronger proof of genuineness.

Such may be offered as a rapid summary of the light in which we are taught by Scripture itself to regard the various books composing the Bible. Christ sets His seal to each of the Jewish divisions of the Old Testament, and promises to His Apostles full illumination by the Holy Ghost in discharging their duties. The Church, beginning from the Apostles' time, carefully sifts the evidences for the genuineness of inspired writings, rejects a considerable number, and, after investigating the claims of some which were not so generally known, and hence were doubted, makes use henceforth of our New Testament books, and the Old Testament, as the only works laying rightful claim to full inspiration.

So far I have left untouched the question: "What is inspiration?" To answer it let us look again at the facts. What seems the object of these books? What is their general character? Are the historical books full in their narrative? By no means. Beginning with the creation, they confine themselves almost at once to the history of one comparatively small portion of the human race. The circle narrows and narrows, with only an occasional glimpse of what is going on outside it. The history of only one family is carried down to the Deluge. When the world begins again, the same process strikes us; until at last and definitely, we find Abraham's family occupying the entire canvass. Thenceforward, till the division of the Jewish monarchy, and beyond it, only the chosen people engross our attention. But we have by no means a consecutive account even of them. Great gaps occur, embracing many years, for which we are referred to the chronicles of the kingdoms. Important wars are only incidentally mentioned. What *is* fully related, and related too, in two separate works, is the *religious* history of the people, and what has any, even remote, bearing upon it. The worldly wisdom or unwisdom of this policy or that, though plain to a child, is not commented upon; while the religious element, as the cause of prosperity or of reverses, is everywhere predominant. It is plain that this, and only this, is the prime object of the history, whether compiled from public or private documents or, so to speak, original. The same thing is apparent in the poetical books. Whether they are filled, like the Book of Proverbs, with the application of God-fearing common sense to the duties and the difficulties of every-day life, or embody, like Job, the profound questionings of a great soul struggling in the abyss of doubt, and emerging triumphantly and humbly at last into the mountain air of faith; whether as in the Song of Solomon, the strength

and purity and constancy of wifely love be the subject, or
as in Ecclesiastes, the hollowness of sensuality, ambition
or *mere* culture,—the impotence of aught, save the fear of
God and obedience to His commandments, to satisfy the
most gifted soul; — or again, as in the Psalms, the whole
range of spiritual truths and emotions, public and private,
past, present and future, individual and national; — whatever be the theme, it always is one that finds its place
within the generous limits of *divine truth*, in its direct
application to the immortal spirit of man.   The Prophets
and the Books of the New Testament are hardly more
truly, though they are more distinctly, directed to this
one end.   General history, military history, national history as such, is not aimed at : the royal archives exist only
in extracts in books that have another object; the book
of the wars of the Lord has been allowed to perish.
Scientific truth is not the object : Solomon's book of
botany has been lost.   The preservation of national bal-
lads, or even religious poems, is not sought: of the book
of Jasher we have only a few fragments.   Nothing then,
which is distinctly appropriate to such objects need be
looked for in the Bible; you are not to demand treatises
merely historical, ethical, scientific, or literary; you are
not to wonder at its being said that the sun rises and sets,
or stands still.   According to the current conceptions of
men, not according to scientific demands, will the language
be shaped ; and however the miracle of Joshua may have
been performed, it was a miracle, and is told in the most
natural way.   You are not to expect that the Greek of
the New Testament should be the purest Athenian Greek;
it is in the dialect used by those for whom it was
written.   The Bible claims only to be the voice of God

speaking infallibly to the soul of man ; and, while we may expect that it shall be truthful always, *in reason,* we are not to demand that it shall reveal the true theory of the solar system, or anything of the kind.   It speaks honestly, although it speaks according to men's common notions of what we call science.   Religious truth alone being its object, it speaks authoritatively and finally on that.   It does not profess to give you, in that respect, a certain amount of truth, mixed with an indefinite quantity of error.   The way in which Christ and His Apostles treat the Old Testament is the way in which we are to treat both the Old and the New Testament.   Infallible moral and religious truth is revealed in them by God.

But the question with which I began recurs here.   How are we to explain the difference of style in different parts? How can styles so different be all the direct inspiration of the Holy Ghost?   St. Peter's words are the fullest answer to this, and the fullest proof of the way in which, as I have just said, the words of the Scripture at large are to be regarded. " Prophecy came not in old time by the will of man, but holy men of God spake as they were moved by the Holy Ghost."   The supposition of a mere general impulse to write or speak what is *in the main* truthful, will not allow us to treat the Bible as Christ treated it, with reverence for its very *words*.   And yet the manifest working of individual minds, character, education, shows that the Holy Ghost made use of these, and did not treat Isaiah, or St. Paul, or St. John as *mere* instruments, having nothing to do with the message delivered by them.   Here, then, we have two sets of facts : on the one hand, judging by Christ's treatment of the Old Testament, the verbal inspiration of the Bible ; on the other, the free working of individual peculiarities. I do not pretend to say how these two facts co-exist; I only say they do co-exist, and that he who overlooks either is cutting away the foundation on which the other reposes. To quote the words of a theologian of whom our diocese and the Church at large may well be proud, "The nature of inspiration is this— a miraculous impulse from the Holy Ghost to write certain things, reaching on in its controlling influence to the accomplishment of the writing of Scripture itself, bringing into exercise and using all the powers, acquirements and activities of the human writer, leaving his individual characteristics, both intellectual and moral, in full play; yet always so as to secure that the result shall be infallible truth; that the Word written shall be properly 'the Word of God.'"

How to understand so peculiar an operation, I do not pretend to tell. Prophecy is but another form of the same mysterious activity of the Holy Ghost. Admitting it, we admit the principle of verbal inspiration. But we are not, I hope, to learn to-day that Revelation is a mystery, nor to see why it must of necessity be a mystery. We should only ask to know what the record itself tells of its source, of its character, and of the respect we owe to it. Let me say in closing that it assures us by its general tenor, as well as by specific declarations, that all Scripture is given by inspiration of God. Our Saviour showed us how we are to revere its very words. We see in it the revelation which it purports to give of the past and the future. We find it "quick and powerful, and sharper than any two-edged sword, piercing even to the dividing asunder of soul and spirit, and a discerner of the thoughts and intents of the heart." And yet in this complex message we discern no less clearly the voice of Paul, of John, of Job. We are concerned not so much to have a clear understanding of how all this comes to be, but only how we may at the same time reverently hearken to Him whose Almighty Word chaos and darkness heard and took their flight, and also may hear speaking with us face to face the holy men of old whose tones come to us unmingled through all, like two opposite currents of electricity through the one invisible cable, sunk into caverns of the mysterious ocean.

II.

THE CHRISTIAN STANDARD.

"I say, through the grace given unto me, to every man that is among you, not to think more highly of himself than he ought to think; but to think soberly, according as God hath dealt to every man the measure of faith."—Rom. xii. 3.

THE direction things are taking in the world has many consequences, not at first, nor to every man, clearly discernible. Look where we may, we find that governments are beginning to give to all classes of people a larger and more direct share in the management of public affairs. Even where the course of history for hundreds of years has been towards oppression, we find that more humane and enlightened principles begin to be acted upon. Russia frees her millions of serfs hardly better off than were our own negro slaves ten years since, and admits them to the class of citizens (for the present condition of things can hardly be more than temporary). As the result of a long and terrible civil war, our slaves take their place as American citizens, and whether capable of discharging their new duties or not, have those duties allotted to them. Prussia, England, Spain, all are moving in the same direction—that which removes from human beings the old fetters by which they were bound, whether the chains be simply deprivation of political rights and privileges, or actual servitude. And we ourselves, whether wisely or unwisely, time will show, have opened all offices to public competition, have left everything that could possibly be

15

left, to the decision of the people at the polls, making the most ignorant and incapable man of just as much importance there, as we make him who is most fully qualified to judge the questions of the day with calmness and impartiality.

Such, no doubt, is the direction in which things are drifting throughout the civilized world : what is to be the end of it God only knows. But in the meantime there are certain consequences resulting from this state of affairs which are unquestionably good, while there are certain others which are as unquestionably bad. Among the former one must be aware of an increasing self-respect on the part of him who is thus made, politically, the equal of others, *provided* he has the elements of a manly character within him. Air and sunlight are not more wholesome for a tree than are liberty and equality for an honest, energetic and capable man. Then again, in rural districts at least, sharing in political rights and duties, enlarges a man's life. It gives him other and larger things to think and act about, than are to be found among his scattered neighbors, or among the affairs of his own narrow community. As we find it in this country more particularly, where newspapers are so plentiful and so widely read, no unprejudiced person need doubt that the possession of a vote tends to elevate and enlarge many a mind that would under other circumstances have lived its allotted years hardly on a higher level than that of the brute. The peasantry of some European countries as compared with the nearest corresponding class among us, may be taken as sufficient proof of this.

So much for one side of the matter. But on striking the balance, we find that we must take into account a great many other things, ordinarily lost sight of in our more enthusiastic moments of pride in the institutions of America—things calculated to lessen very greatly our contempt for other countries and their systems. We find for instance, that a terrible deal of corruption is caused by making a vote so common as to give its possessor little or no pride in it. The utter ignorance of a large proportion of voters, again, is the reason why impostors and scoundrels make them so easy a prey, while really honest and competent men, unless they devote their lives to politics, must, as a general thing, stand in the background, because they cannot, without losing their self-respect, condescend to practice the crafty, sneaking acts of the professional politician. All these things, and many more of the same general kind, need to be always remembered by every American citizen, lest he should be overmuch puffed up by what is really fitted to arouse patriotic pride, and especially, lest he should think that politics can do without his own informed, honest interest and activity.

There is, however, one other consequence of which I must speak, because it connects what I have said with what I have to say. It has a certain influence, no doubt, upon politics; but only in the sense that what a man is must affect all his actions. It is this: finding himself the equal *at the polls*, of every and any one else, however prominent otherwise, many a man thinks himself equal to all others in every way. If the question be one of large and general interest, the man who has not an idea, or a principle, counts for as much as another who is intelligent and cultivated, and hence arises very often, a brutal desire to exercise his power simply in order to annoy a neighbor who is envied on account of superior wealth. Even where this low and coarse jealousy does not exist, there is a great temptation to undervalue those things which really make one man another's *better*. I do not feel called upon —no man is called upon—to respect another for his money alone. That is one of the most contemptible and debasing things in the world. But the *qualities* which commonly result in the acquisition of money, these, if honesty be among them, are worthy of all honor, in their proper place. In a word, *character*, goodness, honor, enterprise, truthfulness are worthy of respect; and he wholly misunderstands the meaning of our boasted American equality who thinks, as so many of us seem to think, that because one *vote* goes for as much as another, therefore one *man* must be the equal, in other things, of all others. Especially is this ridiculous and short-sighted disposition noticeable in regard to other qualities, which are not even so readily tested in their practical effects as those of which I have been speaking. Industry, thrift, and so on, generally make so plain a mark, and bring in so rich results, that no man can help acknowledging their value to a certain point. But there are other qualities which are even more worthy of respect than these, inasmuch as they have still more to do with making a finished and complete character. Education, refinement, courtesy, are among these; and, for myself, I must say that these arouse far higher respect in my mind than those faculties which simply enable one to make money. Sometimes even these are recognized as they should be; but as a general thing, I think every thoughtful person must admit that among the coarsest, the most ignorant, the most narrow-minded of our people there is a disposition to think and talk as though they were fully equal to any of their fellow-citizens—to pronounce opinions on things they know nothing about—to take even a pride and satisfaction in showing to every one that they do not admit any living man to be their superior. Wherever this temper is called out by airs of superiority not justified by facts, it may be excused; there are few things more foolish or more ridiculous than such pretensions when not grounded on real goodness and merit, which is precisely the case in which you never see them.

What I have been aiming at all along is to show that our political system gives strength to a disposition which human nature has already quite strongly enough—the disposition to think more highly of one's self than one ought to think—to undervalue those things which really give a claim upon our respect and admiration. But that which is the immediate cause of it all is the want of a proper standard by which to judge of what makes a lofty and noble man. Without this, no discipline can make us noble. With this, we shall be doubly elevated in our characters; for there is nothing better fitted to ennoble a man than genuine respect for what is good; while this requires as its condition, a correct notion of what good is.

Now in the text, the Apostle Paul gives us a very clear notion of what this standard is. The Roman Christians to whom he was writing, appear to have become involved in a very childish dispute about the prominence to which each was entitled. It was childish; and yet it was just such a matter as men often get involved in, for want of that true standard of goodness and merit without which very absurd things monopolize a deal of the world's regard. You remember that in that early age of the Church, when multitudes could recollect the day of Pentecost, and the descent of the Holy Ghost in flame upon the Apostles, there was a class of divine gifts or " charisms " as they were called, very frequently bestowed by the Spirit of God upon members of the Church—gifts which gradually ceased after the Apostles' death. Some of these, though not all of the most remarkable of them, are mentioned in the chapter from which the text is taken. Among them were prophecy, gifts of healing, and performing other miracles, and the power of speaking languages they had never learned (though the person who spoke them did not, ordinarily, *understand* what he said, but it had to be translated for the edification of the people by some one else, who, like the other, did not understand the language except when under the immediate influence of the Spirit). Now the persons thus honored began, it would seem, to take undue pride in these gifts, and to think, each one, that he was superior to the rest. Forgetting that these powers, just like the grace which had regenerated his soul, were the free and undeserved gift of God, they became puffed up, and no longer thought soberly of themselves as they ought to think. Therefore St. Paul found it necessary quietly to rebuke them, and show them where they were making a grievous mistake. He pointed out that great Christian truth, of which we, too, need often to be reminded, that the Church was like a body, which must have a great many different parts in order to do its work effectually, and that, instead of contending for superiority, they should rather feel that each was closely connected with every other. In harmony and love, not in wrangling and disputing about position, they were to do God's work and save their own souls. But if (or since) they must have a standard, let them remember that he was the greatest among them who had most *faith*. Not the man who spoke most strange languages when under the special influence of the Holy Ghost, not the man who could most eloquently expound his neighbor's unknown message from on high, not he who could heal most diseases, or who could see most clearly what was going to happen to the Church—none of these was entitled to the highest place of honor; but he who believed most heartily in God, and clung to his Divine Father with the most sincerity and consistency. *He* was the best Christian, and as such, was the man to honor. In proportion as a man had this gift of faith, he might make himself easy about precedence and place. He would find in God all the comfort and pride that it was good for him to have.

What was sound advice for the Roman Christians in the first century, I suppose will fit us quite as well in the nineteenth. If we are inclined to make much of ourselves —to think that we amount to a good deal more than any body else—if we find in ourselves a disposition to criticize and pull to pieces what everybody is doing because we are so very, very wise—if we undertake to pass our solemn judgments on religious, or Church, or political matters that we have never studied and know nothing particular about, when people who have devoted much time and attention to them give opinions differing from what we happen to fancy—under all these various circumstances it may easily be that we are not simply making fools of ourselves, but likewise, are encouraging in our souls something that will make it much harder for us to enter the Kingdom of Heaven. It is not only because Christ said so that we feel that undue pride stands terribly in the way of true spirituality. Our every-day experience shows that it has a similiar influence in hindering us from getting any good qualities we may have into working order. We do not work patiently to find out the truth of something; we jump hastily at an opinion; and whatever we first think, hit or miss, must be right because we have thought it, or caught it. We can never grow any wiser, because we think we already know everything that is worth knowing. We cannot join in anything where we have not the first place; and so we join in nothing at all. Hold a pin's head close enough to your eye, and you will find that it hides from you a great number of things a good deal larger than you are. So this foolish pride and self-esteem kills your spiritual life by making everything else seem small, and by giving birth to the feeling that if you cannot be at the head you will do nothing.

See how finely St. Paul's advice meets this danger. We are to measure ourselves and our importance by our faith. Now no man can have true faith who has not at the same time a deep feeling of his own weakness and sinfulness. Ask yourself what times have been fullest of spiritual joy and trust. Were they not precisely those periods when you felt most humble—most capable of throwing your whole self into the arms of God, and asking him to do with you as he thought best? Does not your soul get heavier—do you not find prayer and meditation harder, when you are satisfied with yourself, and have lost that deep feeling of the absolute necessity of being continually bathed in the atoning blood of Christ? No answer but one can be given to these questions by any man who knows from his own experience what religion is. We can lay it down as a universal rule, that when a Christian is humble, then he is growing; when he is puffed up, then his growth toward God is very feeble or utterly at a standstill.

There is, of course, such a thing as understanding what you know, and what you can do, and taking an honest pride in the capacity which God has given you, and which you have patiently cultivated, to the best of your ability. There is likewise such a thing as independence, and a determination to hold your own against people who would (as we say) "impose upon" you. They are both things which are important to true manliness and worthy of all respect. But they are also very easy to push too far. And the best means of avoiding that mistake, is to cultivate Christian *faith* which rounds and completes the character, because it brings us more into the likeness of Him who is the model on which our lives are to be shaped. With a deep feeling of our dependence upon God we can run but little risk of thinking too highly of ourselves on account of what He has given us. With true love for Christ, there will arise of itself a love towards our fellow-creatures, which will instruct us, better than any formal rules ever can, what are our rights, and above all, what are our *duties* towards them. We shall solve many a difficulty, and avoid many a snare, by fixing our attention not so much on what is due to us, as on what is due to others, and especially to Christ.

I have spoken of the effects upon ourselves of cultivating humility and faith in our own souls. But there is another matter directly connected with the subject, which may fairly enough have been in St. Paul's mind when he wrote the words of the text. And that is the matter of our standard of judgment, not only for our own lives but for human life in general. The two are, indeed, very closely connected. He who makes the attainment of spirituality the great aim of his own life will not be apt to lay too much stress upon the extent to which others have won prizes inferior to that. But still, it is of sufficient importance to be dwelt upon for a few minutes,—the effect of making this the rule by which he shall estimate what people are so busy about in the world.

It is enormously difficult : that is the first thing that strikes us. The prizes of life are so often won by men that have faith in very little which we can call wholly good, and their success is so brilliant and dazzling, that it needs, in many a case, a decided struggle before a man can deliberately put the two together and decide which is seriously the more desirable, worldly success and no faith, or faith and little or no worldly success. But there is not much genuineness about anyone's Christianity who finds it too much for him to do. In its difficulty, to tell the truth, lies a great deal of its importance. To succeed in making the choice in the depth of your own heart, and not for the purpose of *saying* so, is itself to have won a pretty complete victory over one of the strongest positions the Devil holds in your heart. By any one who has deliberately made the choice, an immense advantage is gained. In the first place, he is no longer exposed to a vast number of the most subtle and dangerous forms of temptation, which, if yielded to, very surely eat out all the nobleness and purity of his Christian character. He will be free from envy,—that basest and most harmful sin; he will be free from worldliness in its various forms, dragging down the soul from the heights to which the divine love has lifted it, and besmirching its pureness with the mire and filth of greed and covetousness, and every hateful meanness. And on the other hand, he will have set before him an ideal which will be forever shedding down its kindly influence upon his endeavors after better things. One or two such people many of you know, and you know likewise, that to sit and talk with them for half an hour gives you strength to quell your lower nature, and sends a flush of health and vigor through the best part of you such as a plunge into a cold bath sends tingling through every nerve of your body. If such be the effect of a simple determination to estimate things by their religious, or true side, when you meet with it in another man, what must not its force be when generally adopted as your own standard! Any one who has ever tried it may answer. It so marvellously strips away their attractions from the objects that tempt us, but which in our inmost hearts we know to be beneath the notice of our immortal souls—it so stimulates us in the pursuit of holiness and God—it so firmly and yet so kindly rebukes us when we are inclined to go astray, that we know it to be an inspiration from Heaven, sent to make the upward path easier for our sluggish feet.

To have such a *standard* by which to measure the thousand pursuits that are constantly pressing themselves, uncalled, upon our attention, is a great help towards forming a judgment about them which will cleanse and raise our souls. As such, dear friends and fellow-Christians, I present it to you. Throughout our busy lives we all need something that may humble us, and cause us to hunger after the spiritual food that is to be gotten from God alone. We shall be tempted to think of ourselves and our doings with undue pride—to forget the hole and the rock whence we are digged—to think of what we are as the result of our own exertions. On the other hand, from the tone of the world

2

around us will come only too many allurements to set up
the success which is measured by money and influence as
the great end of human life.   From both dangers we may,
through God's help, be freed by adopting as our Christian
motto this admonition of St. Paul: " Think of yourselves
soberly, according as *God* hath dealt to every man the
measure of *faith*."   Let us carry it away with us then
to moderate our foolish self-sufficiency, to give us a worthy
and Christian standard of action, and to inspire us with
the strength that comes from living as men should do
who stand in the constant presence of " Him who is invisible."

III.

THE BURNING BUSH.

SIXTH SUNDAY AFTER TRINITY—FIRST LESSON.

" And Moses said: I will now turn aside and see this great sight, why the bush is not burnt."—Ex. iii. 3.

WHATEVER differences there may be in other respects as to our view of human life, no one who has had any large experience of it has failed to learn that one of its many needs is the power to endure the ills (as we call them) with which it is rife. This has been the aim of all the philosophies that have swayed the world. Men have attempted, like the Stoics of old, to attain this power by persuading themselves that ills were not ills, but only disguised blessings; a principle whose truth it is possible fully to make our own only by connecting with it the beliefs which Christianity affords. Another method of reaching the same end has been tried in the distant East by Buddhism, with its teaching that human suffering is but the punishment for sins committed in a previous state of existence, and that the goal to which we shall finally arrive is an unconsciousness so deep that all our earthly sufferings will be forgotten in that painless slumber to which the good may look forward.

Or, still again, we find the deep tendency to fatalism which lies at the bottom of many a man's belief, erected into a system like that of a great German writer of recent times, calling upon the power of resistance which is so valuable a part of our nature, and exhorting men to bear simply because all these purposeless ills of life are unavoidable, and that it is base to sink under them in weak dejection and despair.

Fortunately for the ongoing of the world, we do not think much of this dark question, save when it is forced upon us by the evils of our private lot. It is really one of the most wonderful things about our strange human nature that we should be able so largely to throw off the weight which, if it incessantly bore upon us, would make existence an unendurable burden. Look out over the world, and see what an appalling amount of misery, degradation, pain of body and of mind, meets your gaze on every hand; and you are almost ready to despise yourself for being able to draw a happy breath. In certain moods, to one at least who has had his power of sympathy cultivated by exercise, the burden does seem one which is capable of darkening every life. And although the wise providence of God has made it possible to throw off this weight when we are not immediately engaged in the work of relieving misery, every life has in it calls amply sufficient to make us feel the need of some comprehensive view of the matter which may guide us aright in meeting, and what is more, in preparing for the calamities which are always springing up unexpectedly, and from the most unlooked for quarters. Each one of those ways of reconciling ourselves with the ordinary lot of man, to which I have referred, was not the idle dream of an abstruse thinker, busying himself with airy problems which could never have any bearing upon life, but the attempt to meet, and satisfactorily to deal with a question of supreme practical importance. It is a question too, which, while pressing upon humanity in all ages with greater or less power, becomes more and more in need of an answer according as increasing intelligence and education enlarge the horizon of men's lives. All through the literature of the past we find the sad under-current of wonder and perplexity over the prevailing misery of human life. From the book of Job to the serious utterances of our own day it stands out clearly or dimly, as the subject to which more thoughtful minds are drawn by an inexplicable fascination. And the necessity of settling it is more widely felt as, in various ways, men come to feel nearer than they used, to distant quarters of our globe. The Indian famine, whose terrors were so nobly mitigated by the exertions of the English authorities, came before us with appalling force, and entered, as two centuries ago it could not have entered, into the great total of facts which must be explained. The slave-trade in Africa, with all its desolating horrors, instead of looming up dimly in the distance, almost, of another world, is revealed by such men as Livingstone and Baker, and every reflecting mind, as well as every civilized government, is called upon to deal with it as a question of either practical or speculative moment.

So far as the practical treatment of such matters is concerned, we may be convinced that the world is alive to its necessity now, perhaps, more fully than ever before. It has come to be admitted on all sides that governments have a duty in dealing with such questions, and one whose limits are not determined by the amount of harm that is done to their own citizens. In the private treatment, if I may so express myself, of misery and want, there probably was never so much intelligent and active exertion as we see around us every day. But the way to meet trouble in our own case is a problem ever new, and ever demanding a solution.   To me, the solution which is afforded by the Christian revelation is one that seems to meet the difficulty, so far as it presents itself as a matter of speculation.   The cause of suffering—sin; the purpose of suffering —purification; the distributer of suffering—an all-wise Father; the reward, or rather the fruit, of patient suffering —an eternity of spiritual growth and progress; these answers, many of them grasped by the human mind long before their full revelation in Christ Jesus, now have been stamped as true by the seal of God Himself; and we have to deal with only the details of the question.   And let us not fancy that, because these details are hard to understand, therefore nothing has been gained by having these previous questions and principles settled.   It is hard for us to put ourselves, as Christian men, into the state of mind to which it is an open question whether there be a divine Father.   It is difficult for us to imagine the blackness of mental darkness which would be produced by absolute uncertainty whether there be a conscious life hereafter. Compared with the hopeless character that would be imparted to the question by total ignorance on points like these, what we have to deal with is of very minor difficulty. And indeed, to a true Christian soul, the only real difficulty is that of demeaning himself under his own trials as his beliefs demand that he should.   What I mean, of course, is not that sympathy and pain are not the feelings with which he views the misery of others, nor that the influence of the religion of love is not directly to deepen his sympathy with sorrow, and increase his desire to lessen it. All that I mean is that the speculative difficulty—the blank perplexity with which human suffering would be viewed by one who did not believe in an all-wise and fatherly Providence of God,—has no place in the mind of one who does so believe. Such a belief, like the major premise of a syllogism, necessarily involves the conclusion that human suffering has a purpose, and one that not only justifies its existence, but would actually convince us, were our vision strong enough to perceive it, that God's father-liness is shown in that very arrangement of affairs which now appears to cast doubt upon it. This, I suppose, is what every thinking Christian falls back upon. And the apparent superiority in reasonableness of those who object to such a way of solving the difficulty lies, after all, only in this, that they decline to fall back on any thing, or in other words, have no explanation at all that can satisfy the moral sense.

But still, there remains the difficulty of settling it for one's self, which is a task for the character rather than for the mind. I may have no trouble in mentally referring my own suffering, or the suffering of others, to God's wise and loving discipline. But it is a question in which are summed up most of the perplexities of living a Christian life, how to learn this lesson so thoroughly that we may *act* upon it, and make it the habitual temper of our mind and soul to *feel* that God doeth all things well.

In saying that in this problem most of our other religious difficulties are summed up, I necessarily decline any attempt to deal *all at once*, with them and with their remedies. I propose to speak to-day of only one of these: it is the one that appears to be suggested by the story which was read as the first lesson for the morning. After the failure of his first attempt to free his brethren from the yoke of Egyptian slavery, Moses retired, in bitter disap-

pointment we may be sure, to the lonely desert lying
around Mt. Sinai, seeking in a herdsman's duties at once
the relief of action, and leisure to meditate upon his failure
and its cause.   Whatever balm to his wounded spirit may
have been possible from tender earthly ties, he seems to
have found in his family life, which now began; and if we
may infer from her name anything as to his wife's character, and capacity to lighten the burden of disappointment,
we may imagine that he found in her, in far greater
degree, the strange relief from care, the deep remedy
for bitterness which other great minds have found in the
touching innocence and affection of a pet bird; for such is
the beautiful significance of the name by which she is
known to us.   But the history does not allow us to suppose that he was diverted from his grand purpose by this,
or by any other alleviation which he may have found upon
his path; although the influence is incalculable that may
have come to him, as to so many others of the world's
greatest characters, from the softening and ennobling of the
nature which God seems to have connected, for so large a
portion of our race, with the family relation.   Softened and
ennobled he certainly was, by this or some other influence;
for when he is again brought before us, he is fitted for the
work which he had previously failed to achieve.   The story
of the burning bush is too well known to need that I
should repeat it, even had it not just been read.   The use
to which I mean to put it, is not that for which it was
first meant, but one for which it has always seemed to
me particularly fitted.   The *truth* to which it was meant
to draw Moses' attention was that of Jehovah's endless
and unchanging being, and the *lesson* to be derived by
him was faith in the promises long before made to Abra-

ham, that his descendants should come up out of Egypt into the land in which he was then a sojourner. The purpose to which I would reverently apply it is to illustrate the moral uses of the Christian endurance of trial.

For, as I have said before, our difficulty as Christians, is not the framing of a theory by which we may still the *mental* unrest aroused by the spectacle of human suffering, our own or that of others, and reconcile its existence with the fatherliness of God. The mind is too well convinced, by looking back upon its own history and watching the beneficial result of trial patiently endured, that the purpose of suffering, and its natural effect are good, and worthy of such a God as ours. What we want is the moral power to take patiently now, once more, the chastisement that comes to us. We want the ability, now that sickness, or bereavement, or poverty, or neglect is buffeting us, to turn the check to the smiter in resignation—nay, in thankfulness. We want in short, to translate our creed into the language of action and endurance.

More than this, too, we want, if our horizon be not terribly narrowed by selfishness. We desire that not in our words alone, not alone in our demeanor when prosperous and healthy and honored, but likewise in that speech which is the most eloquent, as well as the hardest to learn, in the endurance of adversity, to utter our testimony to the power of Christ in changing the soul from what it is by nature into the fulness of His holiness. This must form a part of every Christian's ideal. If one member of the Lord's body, the Church, suffer, without being benefited, by the discipline to which it is subjected, all the members suffer, if not by positively being harmed, yet at least, by being deprived of that most salutary of lessons, the

2*

spectacle of faithful endurance. Our responsibilities under this head, toward each other, are second only to those we have toward God Himself. For how shall men hear unless they are addressed? And what form of communicating truths like these can for a moment be compared in effectiveness with the mute eloquence of a soul crushed by trial yet crying: "Though he slay me, yet will I trust in him?"

The influence on Moses of the sight that he witnessed is only an example of the truth that what is addressed to the eye in outward deed far surpasses in its influence that which is addressed only to the mind. One would have thought that the long story of God's dealings with His chosen would already have branded upon Moses' mind the lesson of His unchanging faithfulness. To what, if not to this, was testimony borne by His choosing Abraham, and His slow working out in his descendants, thus far, of the purposes announced to the Father of the faithful? The very captivity in Egypt was not left out in the clear unveiling of Israel's destiny that was made to Abraham, under the starry Chaldean skies, when the horror of great darkness fell upon him, and he was assured that God would be his shield and his exceeding great reward. Yet, for all this, it was needful to impress upon Moses, as though he had never learned it before, the lesson that amidst appearances the most contradictory, God's slow-rolling purposes were accomplishing themselves. The sight of the bush, burning with fire, yet unconsumed, must bring back the faith which the history of long generations had failed to make strong enough for the test which it must bear.

Who of us can say that his faith would be competent to

grapple with trial were he alone, of all men, singled out to bear it? Would the glorious history of the Church's past suffice to nerve us for the conflict? Would even the spectacle of the God-man, spurning the aid of eager legions of angels, and coping with temptation in that strength which you and I may have for the asking—would even this ensure our victory? I trow not. Therefore it is that by such spectacles as we may behold every day of our lives, the rust is cleared away which perpetually threatens to fill up in every heart the divine inscription that tells us that "Whom the Lord loveth He chasteneth, and scourgeth every son whom He receiveth." Who can reckon the worth of these silent utterances of the voice of God? I think upon my life, with its monotony, its lack of great outlooks, its petty cares, its stunting and distracting worriments, perhaps its sickness, or its poverty, or its contempt, and I think, it may be, that I have ground for an impugning of the justice and the love of God. How can I,—such is the instinctive utterance of the unsubmissive heart,—how can I look for any ripening in religious life, for any fresh understanding of the ways of God, for any realization in my own case, of the calm serenity which breathes through the Gospel of Christ, when mean and paltry irritations are perpetually diverting my attention, when grandeur or sublimity of purpose is constantly interrupted by having to apply myself to providing bread for those dependent upon me,—when, in a word, I live a life which is lit up by no rays of greatness, but is of necessity spent in commonplace duties which no enthusiasm can possibly turn into anything but narrowing influences?

This feeling of hopelessness of doing aught of much consequence is a very common one; and it particularly arises in those cases where there really is the capacity of doing what is of great consequence. But it is *not* done, because men do not rise high enough to take in the importance of every man's duties, whatever they may be, provided they *are his own,* which Christ revealed to all who have ears to hear or eyes to see, when He made immortal the poor widow casting in all her living into the treasury, or the weeping harlot who bathed His feet with her tears and wiped them with the hairs of her head. And because men persist in applying an earthly and false standard to measure the moral importance of acts and duties, He shames us with spectacles that reveal to us the emptiness of our lamentations in as speaking a fashion as that wherein the burning bush disclosed to Moses the truth he had forgotten. Turn your eyes away for a moment from your private griefs, and look about you. There is a woman sick unto death, suffering agony by day and by night, without support, and trusting to the Providence of God for the bare necessaries of life, so far as her own feeble but courageous exertions are unable to procure them, alone in the world, yet with a meekness and saintliness of spirit which rise superior to the most commonplace and, as you would think, degrading environment, bearing agony of body and utter destitution of all that makes life attractive. What do you think of it, and its meaning for you? You think you are shut out from doing anything great or imposing. Is her life great and imposing in the highest sense? And if so, how? How, but by its being an utterly unpretending and almost unconscious exhibition in everyday life, of the triumph of the soul over difficulties which none but a heroic soul could overcome? You think your obstacles really hinder you from being contented; they are nothing compared with hers.

There is nothing in your life to inspire you with enthusiasm. Is there anything in hers? You find it hard to submit, and harder still to look forward with submission. She has absolutely no outlook present or future, from her disease, or from her destitution. Yet she is bright, almost happy, in the intervals of her acuter spasms of agony.

Is this a lesson to shame you out of your unworthy estimates, and nerve you to set about something better than unmanly puling? Then thank God for it. "Put off thy shoes from off thy feet for the place whereon thou standest" is ground made holy by the presence of God Himself. Go down in dust and ashes. Abase thyself before Him for having dared to doubt that He has given thee a chance of glorifying Him. Pray Him that the thought of thine heart may be forgiven thee; and learn that there are lives compared with whose trials thine are as nothing, yet that even there the might of Christ's influence suffices to make of them fields of loftiest spiritual victory.

Add to this the harm to others which results from seeing a man weakly lamenting over the burden appointed for him, instead of quietly taking it up and carrying it in reliance upon Him who ordained it—add the loss to others of the example which, when we fairly look at it, is felt to be so humbling and at the same time so elevating, and it can hardly escape any one, that among the most powerful of the means which God has prepared for our awakening is this of stationing all over our weary world these bushes, burning but not consumed by the fires of divine discipline. It can scarcely be too hard a lesson for any one to learn that in every life there are opportunities in profusion for magnifying the Lord who has bought us with His own precious blood.

Do I need to draw for the arousing and encouraging of fainting hearts, upon the store of strength which may be found in the truth of our immortal being hereafter? We all know how the turmoil of our earthly life tends to drown the voice that speaks to us of the recompense of reward awaiting those who by *patient* continuance in well-doing seek for glory and honor and immortality. The collect for the day brings beautifully before us that vision of true beauty which should correct our tendency to measure the meaning of our lives by standards which have no value beyond the present. Let me repeat its hallowed words, that in our endeavor to make our own lives at once worthy of God and inspiriting to our fellows, we may not fail to remember that they are truly great, not according to their apparent importance now, but according to the extent to which they manifest the qualities that are to make up our being hereafter.

"O God, who hast prepared for those who love Thee such good things as pass man's understanding; pour into our hearts such love toward Thee, that we, loving Thee above all things, may obtain Thy promises, which exceed all that we can desire; through Jesus Christ our Lord."

IV.

MOSES AND HIS MISSION.

DEVOTION TO DUTY THAT DOES NOT LOOK TO THE REWARD.

"And he said, Certainly I will be with thee, and this shall be a token unto thee that I have sent thee: When thou hast brought forth the people out of Egypt, ye shall serve God upon this mountain."—Exodus iii. 12.

NOT inappropriately is the spiritual life called a life of faith. In the sign given to Moses we have a striking instance of the way in which a man is often called upon to do and to suffer in trust, uncomforted through his first stage of action and endurance by outward and visible marks of the Divine Presence, but resting all his hopes on something to come, his assurance of which is itself based upon inner communings with God and proof not plain to others.

We all know something of this. All who have wrought in the divine vineyard have had to draw support and cheer under the burden and heat of the day, from the thought of the reward to be given when its task was done. And yet, in spite of experience—in spite of the oft-repeated lesson that thus faith is most largely developed—it is perhaps one of the commonest sources of discouragement that again and again this treatment is adopted, and we are reminded that the harvest must be sown in tears, before it can be reaped in joy. From this portion of the eventful life of Moses I would fain draw this morning something to abate the evil, and point out the good which flows from the discipline in question.

Observe then, the exact nature of Moses' treatment. A mighty task, one which he had before bootlessly undertaken, was imposed upon him anew. His previous attempt had failed because it was made of his own motion. Throughout the whole of the narrative, whether as given in the preceding chapter or in the address of St. Stephen in the Book of the Acts, we find no trace of God's having *at that time* charged Moses distinctly with it. He supposed indeed, that his brethren would have understood that God by his hand would deliver them, and there may have been, even so early, some divine intimation that such was in the end to be his destiny. But there is nothing to show that, either for his own good, or for any other reason, the attempt then made was by the bidding of God; whether or not, he was now distinctly charged to renew it. The gloominess of the prospect was not disguised. Pharaoh's refusal was certain, though success was guarantied as well. But the task was one before which, apart from the previous failure, one bolder than Moses might well have shrunk back. To deliver, by peaceable means, a subject population of millions from the tight grip of an absolute and powerful tyrant, with nothing to rely upon but promised wonders, was indeed a behest calculated to try his faith. Surely, it seemed, there might be something given *now* upon which to found a rational hope—something unmistakable in its character, to which in after years of struggle he might look back in confident assurance that he was not the dupe of an ocular illusion. Learned as he was in all the wisdom of the Egyptians, familiar doubtless, from his own experience, with the ease with which signs like those which were given him during this interview might be the creation of fancy; to such a man the rod turned into a serpent, and the leprous hand, strange as for the moment they appeared, were hardly the things to revive faith when mocked by doubt, or to stand out in time to come as unmistakable signs that this wondrous scene had really taken place. And, such as they were, the same prominence is not given to them as to the other sign whose promise is our text; and they were expressly intended to persuade *others,* not him. Something hereafter to come is the main thing for him to go upon; and that something is the promise that the now enslaved Israelites should worship on the mountain where he stood.

So God is wont to deal with His children in every age. So He dealt with Abraham in Charran—so He dealt with Jacob, and so, to-day with you and me. When we hear His voice bidding us follow Him, we cannot *know* what is coming to us. That our defeats hitherto have been owing to undue trust in our own fancied strength we guess indeed; but it is a leap in the dark to pledge ourselves to renounce the world, the flesh, and the devil. They have worsted us many times; and our sagest counsellors warn us against being over confident that they will not get the better of us again. The feelings that we have to-day are more like the signs granted to Moses for the present weakness of his faith, than any thing which may hereafter stand out in the retrospect clear beyond cavil. The sign on which God lays, and would have us lay the greatest stress, is His promise of some better thing to come—His pledge that the mission He lays upon us is destined to be brought to a triumphant ending.

Now there is about all this something very different from the way in which we should expect to be treated. It would seem natural and best if we had granted to us, at once, a grace unmistakably divine as were the miraculous gifts vouchsafed for a while to the believers of the early Church—the power, that is, to pray without ever being haunted by wandering thoughts, the gift of banishing and permanently keeping out of the mind the old associations with sin and vanity. Then, whenever difficulty appeared, when doubts arose, as rise they will, about our having really met with God, and talked to Him face to face, we should only have to fall back upon this palpable change in us, and there could be no further question that we had not obeyed a voice which our own ears had feigned. This, I say, or something like this is what we might look for, And instead, we get the promise of a triumph at last of which to-day's failures do not speak in any very rapturous tones of confidence.

Let us try to see why this is. With Moses, the granting of even these subordinate signs, the changing rod, the leprous hand, was only *after* he had, as we may suppose, accepted his mission. True, his doubts are not yet entirely cleared away, but they concern themselves now with the difficulties in the way of executing the behest which he feels to be his own work—the people's unbelief—his own lack of eloquence. And even after these have been done away, his great heart quails yet once more, and he angers the Lord by shrinking from his post of duty. But after all, the victory is won, and won too, in the main, I think the narrative gives us reason to believe, *before* the miracles were wrought,—won on the strength of the promise of the text.

Now let us see whether, after all, it was for his own good wholly—whether, in fact, it did not turn out rather to his hurt, that he was entrusted with these miraculous powers. As means to do that which they were meant to do, to persuade the people, to confound the magicians, to leave Pharaoh without excuse, to bring down upon the doomed land the threatened plagues—for ends, in short, which concerned others, they were important, perhaps necessary, for his stupendous and peculiar task. But in those respects where our task is like his—in regard to his spiritual growth—it was far otherwise. What was the great error of his life, that for which he was destined not to witness the complete triumph of his work? Was it not in consequence of his having been entrusted with the won-der-working rod, and having come to look upon himself as entitled to use it for his own ends, and not at the bidding of God? He seems to have slowly assumed to himself a part of the miraculous power of which it was but the em-blem, instead of remembering his own utter insignificance when thought of as more than the obedient wielder, under special commandment always, of the strange might of God. Otherwise, it is inconceivable that his fatal error could have been committed; and it seems likely that the disregarded bidding to call forth water from the rock by speech, not as before by striking it with the rod, and that with Aaron to share in the miracle (Num. xx. 8—12), was dictated by the knowledge that such was the tendency of the leader's thoughts.

And if all this be so, it is a stern rebuke to us for trying to be wiser than God in the ordering of our souls. It sheds light on the dangers to which we should inevitably be exposed by being entrusted with privileges such as I have suggested, and such as we think would so greatly help us in fighting the fight of faith. It is as great a mistake as to suppose that large doses of alcohol really, and permanently, give greater powers of endurance. On the contrary, as the reaction in the physical system is greater than the temporary energy aroused, so too, we may be sure that the apparent increase of faith from having such powers, would be followed by a decrease of the faculty whose very definition is that it is the substance of things not possessed, but hoped for,—the evidence of things not seen. Suppose that whenever you were upon your knees you could concentrate your thoughts wholly upon intercourse with God, *and that with absolutely no effort.* Leave out of sight the certainty that such a power would pre-suppose the attainment already of a state of perfection, and that even otherwise, devotion so rapturous would absorb all your time and thoughts, leaving none for action or for self-conquest in other ways ; is it not plain that while the feeling of God's presence would, by the very supposition, be utterly unclouded, still Faith, in the sense of trusting God—of, so to speak, willingness to *risk* any thing for Him—would be wholly destroyed? And Faith is the most important part of the Christian character. If one may venture to say so, the attainment of this is the very end and aim of our existence. While in itself not strictly a *merit* in God's sight, this ability to trust Him, so slowly won, and so hard to win, must be that on which His eye rests with more favor than on any other grace, during our probation here. Charity, Love, is indeed said to be a greater. But that is only when we take into account the entire existence of the soul. A stage of being shall come when faith shall lose its office in the present vision of glory. But here, fighting with difficulties, struggling with doubt, not in the calm, serene composure with which old painters have limned for us the features of St. George in his encounter with the dragon, but pinning his very life on successful resistance to doubt's dreadful, grisly onset—so fighting, and so wiping the dust of battle from his at last triumphant brow, I think of no spectacle grander to human eyes or more satisfying to those of God than that of a man of faith.

And this, I say, is what the constant, unearned possession of such gifts would but impair and finally destroy.

And again, with us, as with Moses in his unconscious appropriation of the miraculous powers to himself,—his use of them to accomplish his own will,—would the tendency be strong and disastrous. Why, as it is, we have to be always watching against this danger. Who does not know how the exercise of his special gifts breeds, or tends to breed, a vile self-sufficiency which many a mortification is required to crush. Executive ability, when applied to religious enterprises, the power of persuasion, or eloquence, all of these gifts, when they are exceptionally great, demand this caution, and in the absence of it, breed a conceit which often positively neutralizes, if it does not largely overbalance, all the good which the gift would help a man or woman to accomplish. Even in the private life of the soul, so to speak, an unusual ease and comfort in prayer may beget at last, not thankfulness, but pride. Christian generosity may be the mother of vanity. And let any one of these, from being the fruit of toil, become *permanent*, and require no effort, and you may be sure that to you likewise there will present itself some rock of duty or of perplexity from which you will be sorely moved to try to draw the water of comfort for yourself and others, not in the gentle, quiet way enjoined by God, but by the rude, self-willed means that pride suggests. Over the mind would slowly creep the notion that what you always found yourself able to do, you had *in* yourself the power to do; and the self-assertion would bring down upon you, not indeed, if truly bewailed, a total exclusion from the Promised Land, but much weary waiting among the bleak mountain-tops, gazing wistfully towards the far-off abodes of rest.

I think then, we may be assured that it was for Moses' highest behoof that he was left to give in his allegiance on the strength of a promise which, in itself, made a severe demand on his powers of faith; and that the great error of his life lay in the wilful misuse of the gifts which were bestowed, not for his own benefit, but for that of others. And if any good is to come to us from reflecting on this momentous event in the life of one of the world's greatest characters, it must lie, mainly, in making us more contented in our acquiescence in the way which the Lord has appointed for our growth in grace—the winning, by slow and toilsome effort, the power to *feel deeply*, to *pray devotedly* and to *act successfully*.

But rebuke to foolish and inordinate cravings, here, as always, is not the only outcome of God's dealings with His chosen. Cheer, as well as reproof, flows from them. Rather, as the bitter waters of Marah were made sweet by casting into them the branch that the Lord showed to Moses, so is the apparent neglect of His children sweetened by what God has appointed for those who, like Moses, accept the task assigned them to do.

There was no promise of outward manifestation for himself even in the words of our text. All that was assured was that God would be with him. This might be only in the general way of favoring his measures, supporting them, and granting them final success. Jehovah's purpose seemed to be, so far as any recorded words go, to leave him entirely to himself. For the removal of the people's unbelief he might repeat the miracle of the rod. He might do many wonders by means of it. But for anything beyond this sort of appearance, or companionship, he had no assurance. On that understanding he undertook the task. Surrendering all claim upon the perpetual visible presence and guidance of the Almighty—relying only on the promise that in a general way he might count upon Divine assistance, his sorely-burdened spirit took up the load, which doubts as to his own abilities, only, had ever tempted him to decline. But what was indeed the result? Did God leave him alone to decide upon any measure, or to execute those needed to bring to good effect the mission on which he was despatched? Far otherwise. On none of the Old Testament worthies has the continual dew of God's blessing been so bestowed as upon him who, under the influence of these dark forebodings, so sturdily assumed the allotted burden. Revealing Himself in every emergency—talking with him face to face, as a man talketh with his friend, admitting him on the holy mount to a nearer view of Himself than has ever been vouchsafed to mortal man,—thus did God show Himself better than His word, to one who could undertake to do His bidding on no more solid guarantee than was to be found in the bare promise that in time to come he should see of the travail of his soul and be satisfied. And such revelation, was it an arbitrary reward that might have been withheld or not? Did it not rather link itself with the special faith thus developed? I am sure it must have been the latter and not the former.

From among all the heroes of the faith commemorated in the famous 11th chapter of the Epistle to the Hebrews, Moses is singled out as being pre-eminently the one who by faith endured as seeing Him who is invisible. That is the special property, or prerogative, or office of faith—to have vision of things not seen as yet by man. And accordingly, it was the undertaking of this mission which so strengthened the faith which it tested, that of all the sons of man none has been so close to God, as none has undertaken a work of such critical and tremendous responsibility so purely in a spirit of faith.

What need we then any further witnesses to the deep knowledge of human wants displayed in the treatment of which we are often tempted to complain, the absence of such unmistakable outward approval and guidance as may assure us that each successive step is accompanied by the benison of the Almighty? It is just because we are always so tremulously and faint-heartedly looking about for it, that it does not come. Accept in an honest and good heart the commission with which God has honored every Christian as an agent in enfranchising human souls from the land of Satan and from the house of bondage—steadfastly believe that He who hath promised abideth ever faithful—and the manifestation of the Divine Presence which you crave before you have earned it, *in prayer, in enlightenment, in cheer* will be sure to come. Your eye is bedimmed because you insist on shutting yourself up in the dark chamber of timidity and distrust. Remember the promise of final triumph already vouchsafed in your being made a member of Christ, a child of God, and an inheritor of the kingdom of heaven: pin your faith upon that, and manfully do whatsoever your hand findeth

to do.   Then this hypochondria of the soul will disappear.
The exercise of faith will strengthen it.   The sober, quiet
discharge of daily duty, within your soul and without, will
be rewarded by such clear vision of God as He cannot give
you now only because you hang back from taking the
means that are appointed for acquiring it.

And what, after all, was the promise that so powerfully
affected the destined leader of Israel?   No personal
reward—no promise that in the slightest degree appealed
to vanity or ambition—no prospect of popularity or satisfaction for himself.   Simply the assurance that the mission
he was called upon to undertake should be fulfilled—God's
chosen freed from painful and degrading bondage.   In the
influence of that promise we see distinctly the nature of
the soul that could be so strongly swayed by it—its unsel-
fishness, its readiness to immolate itself if so the designs
of God might be furthered.   His previous ill-starred effort
had been balked, we have reason to suppose, because the
sad experience of life had not as yet sufficiently impressed
upon him the need of single-hearted devotion to a cause
which might bring to him no outward reward.   Now he
is under no delusion on that score.   He has tried the
people and found them wanting.   No human appeals to
their generosity, no attempts to revive in their bosoms the
love of liberty which they should have inherited from
their fathers, the wild shepherds of the desert—none of
these things could be counted upon.   They would be murmuring, stiff-necked, rebellious, unthankful.   And in clear
prevision of all this, simply and solely that God's plan
might be fulfilled, and that His chosen people might enter
upon the first stage of their religious education, he shook
off his doubts and girded himself to the work.   All he

3

wanted was that, whether in spite of themselves or not, whether at the cost of winning their hatred or not, he might free them, and might have the assurance of their future as the people of God in seeing them worship Jehovah on the mountain where he then received his commission as their leader.

What floods of light does this shed upon the temper with which our own endeavors should be made. True, our own spiritual growth and education are inseparably bound up with our efforts to set forward the salvation of all men. You cannot work *faithfully in any sphere, for others,* without having in larger and larger measure the reward of devoted action. But the motives, the prospects, inciting you to undertake any Christian work may be of very various descriptions. It happens, not seldom, that the mere emptiness of one's life—its lack of absorbing interests, leads one to begin a course of activity simply in order to have something to do. There is in most characters of the better sort, a capacity for taking pleasure in the exercise of natural gifts, which may be the controlling interest to a much greater degree than is readily felt to be the case. And wherever such is the prompting and prevailing motive, instead of a pure desire for God's glory and the welfare of men, there you have something which may more fitly be compared to Moses' first undertaking, with its inevitable failure, than with this second beginning on which our thoughts have dwelt this morning. Such natural gratification is inevitable and proper. Moses, doubtless, in his forty years' guidance of the people, must have had an innocent and hearty sense of pleasure in exercising the gifts as a leader of men with which he was so pre-eminently endowed. But with him, on more than one occasion, this very pleasure, or the bitterness when it was disappointed, led him astray; and he was most truly fulfilling his duty when leaping into the breach between the self-willed people and their offended God, and imploring that his name might be blotted out of the Book of Life, rather than that the people should be destroyed for their iniquities. And this, despite occasional relapses into a less noble mood, must, I think, have been the habitual attitude of his mind—pure, unselfish devotion to the great work of delivering and educating the people, and bringing them in safety to the land of promise, notwithstanding their rebellion, and thanklessness, and pusillanimity. Such, certainly, is the mood in which alone we can work successfully. As the task must be undertaken originally, not on the ground of visible and unmistakable signs, but in the faith of a promise hereafter to be fulfilled—as that promise itself is not one tempting to our natural selfishness, so too, the daily cheer and the daily reward that *are* vouchsafed, will be neither reward nor cheer to us, unless we supremely long for them to come in a spiritual way. Take, for instance, the laborer in the field of education. If his aim, however unconsciously to himself, be to have many pupils, a smoothly-working machinery, a triumphant outward success, and if he really find himself prizing his results of this kind more than the growing spirituality and quiet earnestness of those who are under his influence; then this latter harvest is gravely endangered: he will gain results only of the kind which he lays himself out to gain.

The man whose work is in the sphere of what is commonly called benevolence, must not look for more than Moses got of trust, or thanks, or success in elevating the

objects of his bounty and his labor.   Personal satisfaction
is rarely won to a very great extent in these, or any similar undertakings ; and where it comes in large measure it
has a strong tendency to interfere with the acquisition of
that which we were meant to earn first of all.

That is faith.   To gain it is the main reason why we
are called upon at all to work.   In order that we may gain
it, we are not bribed at the outset with the visible rewards
which, if we had them, would hinder the growth of trust
in God by teaching us to look for support down at them,
not up to Him.   For its sake all that is noble in us, our
belief in an eternal love and an eternal right, is appealed
to by the promise that at last, far off, there shall come as
the guerdon of our faithful labor, the everlasting triumph
of love and right.   It is only when, with the full understanding of the task it undertakes, and of the obstacles in
the way of its performance, the soul has weighed and
chosen, that the general promise of aid widens out into far
more than was plainly intimated at first.   The soul that
has deliberately made such a choice is the one to which
the fullest disclosure of the Godhead is vouchsafed.   Its
victory is already won by virtue of this single, true-hearted
act of faith.   Over and above the pillar of cloud by day
and of light by night which guides and shields all men
who are in earnest, Heaven grants to such that intimate
unveiling, that diviner companionship, in view of which the
promise of a coming Messiah took the form that He was
to be One who should be like unto Moses.   And all this
came to him, as it must come to us, in virtue of the faith
which took the glorious promise of God alone, as the
sufficient support for action, the all-satisfying object of
desire, the self-evidencing proof of final mastery.

V.

THE POWER THAT WORKETH IN US.

"He *** is able to do exceeding abundantly above all that we ask or think, according to the power that worketh in us."—Eph. iii. 20.

THIS is certainly a very great and precious promise. The power of God, we are told, is such as to do exceeding abundantly above all that we ask or think. Not, indeed, that our ordinary asking, or our common thinking is such as befits the calling wherewith we are called. Among ourselves, gathered here to-day in the House of God, the ardor of spiritual aspiration is *probably* not what we ourselves feel it should be. The things in God's gift do not impress our imaginations as the matchless splendor of the new Jerusalem smote the mind of St. John the Divine; nor do our longings find vent in such wrestlings of the soul as were witnessed by the silent olives of Gethsemane. But such as they are—such as the experiences of life have made us, sometimes divinely guided to chisel out a noble image, and sometimes acting only as hard usage affects the coin,—such as our prayers and thoughts are, God is able to do far more than we either ask or think. This promise should be to us what the loan of unlimited credit is to one who is hard pushed in his affairs. He is hampered in every business enterprise by the inability to practise that truest economy (in the old sense)—that wise and thorough adaptation of means to ends—that sage provision against loss and accident which requires large

53

outlay at the start. Undertakings in which a keen eye beholds the promise of abundant gain are closed to him, because the necessary risks are beyond his reach. But the generous loan of a millionaire's unlimited credit places him, at a bound, far beyond the reach of hindrances which have hitherto impeded him in his path to success. The golden key opens portals at which sagacity, unaided, would have knocked in vain.

Such is the promise — the declaration of the text. Whatever spiritual enterprise we may have thought of— whatever of self-conquest experience may have made us feel to be necessary—whatever religious heights we may, aroused by another's success, have dreamed of scaling— here is the warrant of success. No obstacle can impede him who is backed by Almighty power. Every Satanic wile must be foiled, every fiery dart of the wicked one must fall blunted against the armor of God with which, if we please, we may be clothed. We have asked but little, it may be, and that timidly, and hardly looking to receive a tithe of what we requested. But here is the warrant for unlimited asking—for requests such as no saintliest soul that ever lived has more than realized in its earthly career. And yet we do not rise, or hardly rise to the level of our Prayer-Book supplications,—scarce able to believe that prayers expressly meant for ordinary, daily use, do not soar into realms that it were impious for us to dream of invading.

Whence comes this strange contrast between what is offered and what is accepted? Is it that we really believe God to be uttering untruths, when He so frankly offers us His boundless might in working out our salvation, and urges us to avail ourselves of it in the unending conflict we have to maintain against the world, the flesh, and the devil ?   Or is it that we do not care to conquer more than we are conquering now,—that our paltry victories fully content us, and we feel as little desire to soar above our ordinary level, as to abandon the solid earth and poise unrestingly above the storm-tossed ocean with the albatross's tireless pinions ?

Some answer there surely must be, and I do not think it is the former.   Sad experience may have convinced us that, as a matter of fact, we shall never attain to complete mastery over our inner weaknesses, or our external foes. But we do not doubt, I hope, that God *has* the power He so unhesitatingly offers to confer upon us.   Nor can we be sure that the second answer is exhaustive for all. Whatever may be the case with many, even of those who have tasted of the heavenly gift and the power of the world to come, it is *not* true that *all* find in indifference the secret of their comparative failure to gain that which is declared in the text to be within their grasp.   With intervals of discouragement and despondency, with moments when they are cast down by the ill success of some real effort, there are many, we cannot but think, who really want to be better and purer and stronger than they are—whose lives are darkened by nothing so much as by the disappointment they meet with in the endeavor to become so.   Where then lies the explanation ?   Why is it, that with boundless power at our command, and even with no deeply-grounded unwillingness to use it, so large a portion of it should be left *unused* as the ordinary experience of Christians would seem to imply ?

The answer, so far as it is not contained in disbelief or indifference, is to be found in the concluding words of the text. God is indeed, so far as His power and His willingness are concerned, able to do exceeding abundantly above all that we do or can ask, or think. There is no difficulty for Him when temptation confronts us, in showing us, side by·side with the allurement, the infinitely sweeter reward to be found in the sense of victory. For Him it is not hard, when we are minded to slumber beside our dying lamps, to make us alert like the wise virgins, "whose lamps are always trimmed, and whose pure hearts keep modest watch." So far as readiness or power goes, on His part, there is no reason why there should not always gleam before our eyes the vision of the Celestial City, in the flood of whose clear light the noisome glare of sin's gaudiest revels should show like the loathsome thing it is. It is for no lack of power or will in Him that harm comes to us. But that power and will are, in conformity to His plans for us, exerted only "*according to His power that worketh in us.*" To display it, no matter how *we* meet it—to flash upon us the true light when we do not steadily care whether we have it or not—to spare us all the exertion, and so to deprive us of all the good, that by the laws of our nature we must *earn* if it is really to *be* good for us—this were for Him to stultify Himself—to elaborate a world for the purpose of educating us, and then put into our lazy hands a key where, without understanding or profiting by a single lesson, we should find mechanically, the answer to every problem, and the solution of every doubt. Under such a futile, self-contradictory treatment,

> " —to our smooth-rubbed soul would cling
> Nor form nor feeling, great or small : "

our natures would remain at last, undeveloped as at the

beginning. The potent tonic, temptation, which we dimly see far back in the cycles of eternity invading Heaven and testing the fidelity of Seraphim and Cherubim, which was needful to perfect the human nature of Christ himself, would have been without fruit, because without reality, to ourselves; and glory and blessedness, a taste for which seems capable of being awakened only thus, would glow before us without awakening a single responsive yearning.

To those who, without at all reflecting upon these deeper necessities of their nature, have grasped the promises of God, such considerations come with very sore disappointment. Before experience showed them their mistake, and while they were still under the impulse by which their Christian course was begun, it seemed that only *wilful* blindness could account for any one's being other than triumphant. Now, under the light of trial they find that victory is no such easy thing as they fancied; and careless whether this very difficulty be, or be not, necessary to give worth to any victory, they throw up the apparently hopeless conflict. They, like those in Christ's parable, receive the word with joy, and having no root, for awhile believe, and in time of temptation fall away; or going thoughtlessly forth, are choked with the cares that, for its own good, beset every spiritual life.

Let us not be so foolish. Let us endeavor to learn thoroughly a secret whose value is great enough for God to think it worth such a price as the death of His own Son, and the unending struggles, from youth to the grave, of those saints whose blood is dear in His sight.

Let us take an illustration familiar to us all. Your nervous system, suppose, is weakened and deranged by any

one of those numerous influences which so swarm in this
hot, eager, yet self-indulgent life of the second half of the
nineteenth century—by excessive mental toil, by anxiety,
by sorrow, by over-taxing the powers of enjoyment. Your
physician orders you a powerful tonic, and tells you just
how you have been trangressing the laws of health.   You
look at the little phial that contains the prescription, and
think exultingly: Here is the remedy for my ailments. No
more sleepless nights—no more wretched days, overspread
by a nameless and indefinable apprehension of evil—no more
shrinking from the common task, once willingly and eagerly
performed, but of late so unutterably wearisome and disgusting.   In that little space is contained the cure for all
that has made my life a burden.   Yes, and so it is, only
under certain conditions.   You cannot derive from it what
you say, truly enough, it has to give you, if you go on
draining your life out by the very practices which have
brought you into your present condition. Above all,
great as is the curative value of the medicine, you can
gain from it no benefit whatever, unless you take it as
you are ordered, so that its subtle virtues may creep in
salutary currents through your system, driving out the
morbid humors that hinder Nature's processes, lending
strength to the over-tasked nerves, and restoring the balance of body and soul.

All this we know very well, often as we choose to forget
it.   And still more forgetful are we in general, of the parallel obtaining between such a medicine, and the medicine
which God, the physician of the soul, bids us use.   In
exact proportion as we allow His power to work within us,
shall we find lying ready to our hand the power without,
by which we may be more than conquerors in every spirit-

ual conflict.   And the reason for this arrangement, un-pleasing as it sometimes appears, lies upon the surface, and is illustrated by our experience in other departments of life.   Almost always, accompanying success, is the temptation to make too much of one's own agency in bringing it about.   Fortunes or reputations, made in reality by a lucky hit, or an unforeseen combination of cir-cumstances, rather than by any special ability,—how familiar are we with the sight of pride and self-sufficiency based upon this sandy foundation!   It is like Louis XIV. blandly accepting as his due the fulsome adulation of court preachers and poets, when his military exploits were mainly confined to appearing when victory was already assured by the genius of Turenne or Condé.   Nor is there any less disposition, but rather more to indulge in a similar illusion regarding our religious advance.   Who does not remember how, when a temptation often yielded to before, has upon two or three occasions been overcome, the trivial victories, whose only chance of becoming the rule lay in unceasing watchfulness, have been immediately laid hold of and assumed to be the beginning of an un-broken succession of triumphs?   Viewed in the light of such displays of our disposition to over-estimate our moral power, it grows quite plain how the working of divine power within us must of necessity be the measure of the help given us,—of the fulfilment of God's promises to us. Picture to yourself the result, were this state of things broken up. Temptations the most subtle, trials apparently the most decisive as to our union with God, would be resisted or endured triumphantly, and all this without even remotely testing the one, or giving evidence of moral power.   Some inexplicable strength would be felt to flow into us without a moment of that which is, indeed, one of the highest manifestations of the soul's true vitality,—the pause before temptation,—the consciousness of weakness,—the deep sense of sin's hatefulness,—the passionate appeal to celestial aid, followed by the spurning of evil, and the close feeling of God's nearness and love which He means should be the consequence and reward of all this. Under such circumstances as I have supposed, however, all this, or as much of it as would still remain possible, would be almost as mechanical,—almost as completely devoid of moral character and consequence as the movement of a locomotive piston on the admission of steam. He who imagines the mere resistance to wrong, preceded and followed by nothing, to be the whole of religion, is wide of the mark, and sorely needs to have his ways of looking at spiritual matters overhauled. He is living far down upon a level lower than that of the barest, baldest unreligious morality. He overlooks completely the nature of the problem, and the relation man sustains towards God. Such a view is a reproduction in another, and even less worthy form, of that materialism which, when dealing with the body and what we call mind, so revolts our highest instincts. And more than this, it leads almost directly and necessarily to a pride that is of itself the most destructive of all defects to a genuinely spiritual life. For however much at sea we may sometimes find ourselves regarding other uses of temptation, we are all, I suppose, agreed as to one point, viz., that whether it be resisted victoriously, or surrender be honestly repented of, it does bring us into closer relations with God. Once separate victory over it from the working within us of the divine Spirit,—in other words, allow me to feel that I am sure of conquering, no matter how little joy I find in God's presence, no matter how little value I set on the Saviour's love or the Spirit's pleading, and then God is practically wiped out of existence so far as my spiritual dependence on Him is concerned. To all intents and purposes, human nature being what it is, every religious history would be a repetition of that which some one has called a "perfect life," but which, despite its relative nobleness, cares not to claim from Jesus Christ *any* atonement, any mediatorship, anything, in short, save the example that success and experience have furnished for even the most self-sufficing strength, before trial has taught it to distrust itself.

And again, as to even the joy of religious life, let us see what would be the effect of disjoining the gift of divine power in the soul from any cultivation on its own part of the affections and dependence which the natural working within us of the divine Spirit would bring about.

St. Paul will seem, to most of us, a very noble specimen of the way in which religion affects *character*. Any trait which we find prominent in him, as the result of his illumination on the one hand, and of his endurance and experience on the other, it would require very clear and convincing reasons to make us think other than the proper working of religion. Now what do we find to be St. Paul's habitual attitude of mind regarding this matter, of which he has given us in the text a striking exposition? Self-reproach, repentance for sin, deep consciousness of natural frailty, of all these we find traces on every page of his Epistles. We find no less marked also, in the mingled mass of his experiences, a noble triumph and confidence in the power of the redeemed soul to master the sin which doth so easily beset us. "Thanks be to God which giveth us the victory." "In all things we are more than conquerors." Such outbursts are met with continually. But how do they affect him? Is this jubilant confidence a confidence of which he is himself the center? Does he impress us as a man who, having laboriously gained the power of quelling sin, now rests serenely upon his hard-won strength, acknowledging indeed his debt to divine grace, yet now feeling but dimly his obligations to it, as we, when we dash off a letter, are but distantly alive to what we owe to our writing-master in childhood?

Utterly different is his tone. Keen as must be the joy to every self-respecting creature at having spurned the wrong and done the right, we are never allowed by the great Apostle to think that this was what gave him the truest, deepest joy. Always the delight is based upon its intimate connection with the inworking Spirit, with the ceaseless interchange of love between himself, the struggling Christian, and the benign Author and Finisher of his faith, looking down well-pleased upon his achievements, and holding forth to his eager sight the crown which was reserved for him. Strike out this element from his exultation and you annihilate it for him. The contrast for him between victory won for and by himself, without this blessed consciousness of Christ's share and interest in it, and victory gained under his eyes, would be the contrast between an endless Arctic summer's day, dazzling the sight with pitiless gleam from unbroken fields of ice and snow, beautiful but hard, cheerless, intolerable,—between this and the green, placid, peace-breathing spring of our own more favored latitudes, where, as you gaze upon the fertile landscape, light and warmth seem visibly translating themselves into verdure and perfume. "We are more than conquerors:" yes, but all is naught unless you add: "through Him who loved us and gave Himself for us." "God giveth us the victory:" but how?—"through our Lord Jesus Christ?"

For a two-fold reason then, unless here the great Apostle's experience is to be regarded as misleading, is our success in using the unlimited grace vouchsafed to us conditioned by the response it meets within us. Without such a response—without seeing in our inner life the main thing, of which outer success is but the indispensable symbol and result, the fullest outpouring of power would make our souls barren, fill us with pride, and so destroy the very thing for which, so far as we can see, trial and temptation are assigned us at all. And in like manner the delight with which a properly conducted religious life should reward us would disappear, leaving us to the not only fruitless, but joyless, prosecution of an enterprise in which the most essential condition of success is that the affections, not the will alone, should be profoundly interested.

Am I mistaken in supposing that the truth conveyed in the text is much needed by us all? Do I err when I think that with many of us the temptation is strong to measure religious growth by outward things which are by no means always connected with it, leaving too much out of view that inner life upon which, in reality, the worth of all external actions depends? We have been, I trust, in conformity with the solemn words we heard last Sunday, "so trying and examining ourselves, (and that not lightly

and after the manner of dissemblers with God, but so) that
we might come holy and clean to such a heavenly feast, in
the marriage garment required by God in Holy Scripture,
and be received as worthy partakers of that Holy Table."
How have we conducted this examination? I fear it has
too often been in a spirit that overlooked the truth announced by St. Paul—in a spirit that thought to measure
religious progress as we measure miles on a turnpike, by
external marks; and not as restoration to health is determined, by the condition within. The former have their
value, and one whose neglect is indicative of an utter loss
of spiritual life : you can never dispense with them, and
say : though I yield to lust and passion and worldliness
without sorrow, yet I am in a cheering condition, and need
not bestir myself to amend my ways. Such self-deception
is horrible and disastrous; but I believe it to be rarer than
the others, and on the whole not so dangerous, because
more certain to be speedily scattered to the winds. But
the other may go on long without an awakening; and it is
against this that I would to-day especially warn you.
Mere habit, shame, a feeling of responsibility, as we daily
behold in lives which make no pretense of being religious,
may produce an *outward* demeanor on the strength of
which, if *that* were all, a man utterly irreligious might
present himself at the holy feast to which you are called.
But, over and above, though unquestionably embracing
this, there must be the consideration of that which Scripture calls " the hidden man of the heart." Ask yourselves
then, not merely how many times you have prayed, but
also and mainly, *how* you have approached the throne of
grace. Inquire not only whether you have kept yourself
from open transgression, but also why,—whether because

you had learned from old, sad experience that you should suffer more in the end from yielding than from resisting, or from the only true Christian reason, that it was hateful to God, ungrateful to Christ, disastrous to your religious condition. In short, let the investigation be not so much how divine power has been used (though this, I again repeat, is also vitally important), as whether corresponding to apparent gains in the breaking up of evil habits and the forming of better ones, there has manifested itself a heartier, more pervasive, more thorough working of God's Spirit within you. If the previous self-inspection has been at all as searching as it should have been, then even though sufficient attention may not have been directed especially to this one point, a little thought may now avail to convince you of your oversight, awaken your feeling of its importance, and arouse within you the spirit in which alone you are rightly prepared to receive the body and blood of the Redeemer. And as you join with me in the solemn confession, you will be prepared to receive with advantage that declaration of the remission of sins which the Father of our Lord Jesus Christ, hath given his ministers power and commandment to make. As I utter those mysterious words I know not with whom they are to take effect. I only know that they can be of use to none but those who, by hearty repentance and true faith are learning more and more deeply that God's power to do exceeding abundantly above all that we ask or think, is ours only according to the power that we welcome and try to have work ceaselessly within us.

VI.

HEARING AND DOING.

"But be ye doers of the word, and not hearers only, deceiving your own selves."—St. James i. 22.

In this first chapter of St. James' epistle there is a close connection of thought, in spite of the surface appearance to the contrary. Referring, it would seem, to some peculiar stress of temptation which had befallen those whom he addressed, or to some doctrine gaining influence among them as to the source of temptation, and the irresistible fatality attaching to it, he points out in the first two divisions of his exhortation, that trial, so closely connected with inward sinfulness, is yet distinctly ordained by God with the most loving of purposes, and then, that grace to improve it is to be sought from Him who is the bestower of every good and perfect gift.

The Christian understanding of the meaning and object of life is the only one which at all meets the difficulties of the subject. This native sinfulness, whence temptation derives its potency, is to be eradicated in only one way. "Of His own will," says the apostle, "begat He us by the word of truth, that we should be a kind of first-fruits of His creatures." By the new birth, always assumed as the starting-point of a life of true moral progress, we were endued with the excellent gift of resistance to sin, and final triumph over it. Yet this same gift, he proceeds, is not to be looked upon as a power working by itself. Quite

66

the contrary. Its very nature, as a regenerating force for the *moral* being, demands not merely the passive acquiescence of the will, but active exertion in improving to the uttermost the opportunities it affords. We are begotten anew, indeed, by the word of truth and for the highest conceivable end,—with the purpose of exalting us to the position of chief among the creatures of God. "But be ye *doers* of the word, and not hearers only, deceiving your own selves. For if any man be a hearer of the word and not a doer, he is like unto a man beholding his natural face in a glass; for he beholdeth himself and goeth his way, and straightway forgetteth what manner of man he was."

It is this noble exposition of one of the most profound of spiritual truths on which I propose to dwell for a while to-day. Nor is it simply as a part of the divine philosophy of the human soul that I propose to consider it,—rather as one to which it behooves us urgently to take heed lest at any time we should let it slip.

There are various appearances at the passing moment which combine to give peculiar cogency to the need of pointing out the evils of a vague acceptance or toleration of Christianity, with no attempt to be more than merely hearers of the Word. It is hard to know in what spirit to regard much of what is currently written and said on the subject of Christ and Christianity. The coarse and vulgar ranting of a century ago was more repulsive, certainly, than the cool and dignified manner of discussing the Saviour's nature and history at present in vogue among those who totally reject His claims to human adoration as verily and indeed God. But whether it were not better for the moral interests of the world that men should

distinctly understand what must be their choice, is quite
another question.   As a matter of mere taste, one would
certainly prefer to study the hostile system of thought
when couched in the glowing and poetical language of
Lecky or Huxley, or in the cool judicial pages of Herbert
Spencer, than in the coarse blasphemies of Tom Paine, or
in the shallow, though earnest, caricatures of Voltaire.
But the point I am insisting upon is this: Christianity
must be true or false,—Christ must be truly God, or a
shallow enthusiast, if not a conscious impostor.   Either
He was miraculously born; and miraculously rose from the
dead, or else He was guilty of advancing claims both
blasphemous and foolish.   Either He should be adored, or,
with whatever pitying regret over his fanatical self-deception, He should be placed with Mohammed, Joe Smith,
and Joanna Southcote.   For, unless we are to pick and
choose according to no principle, but only by mere whim,
among the statements of the New Testament, He certainly
did put forth claims which no merely human being, in his
right mind, could honestly have advanced.   He who said:
" I and my Father are one," and " He that hath seen me
hath seen the Father,"—who made no attempt to explain
away what the Jews understood to be the claim to make
Himself equal with God,—this person can properly be
made the object of no regard midway between adoration
and contempt.

Now it is in its tendency to obscure this issue that I
find so much to object to in the decent and popular talk
and writing of the day among unbelievers.   Starting, so
far as can be seen, with no critical principle but a disbelief in miracle, they reject the entire Gospel of St. John,
as written too long after Christ's death to give us any

trustworthy account of His character. They reject, as additions for which the Evangelists and tradition alone are responsible, every thing in the other Gospels which implies Christ's Godhead: and all this only, for the most part, because it strikes them so,—because they feel sure that so and so must be a later addition; and in the teeth of all possible evidence from Christian writers, in quotation and reference, reaching down, at the very least, to some years before the death of the Apostle John. And then, having attempted thus to deprive Christianity of any historical foundation, they pick and choose among the fragments that are left, to manufacture an ideal picture of Christ which shall present no features but such as a singularly good man may have presented, and patronize Him as a very noble and admirable type of human character. In this way it is that by vague assertions, and denials quite as dogmatic as have ever proceeded from the pulpit, they contrive to blind men's eyes to that issue of which I have been speaking. People who have been impressed with the Gospel account of our Lord, and have had strong impulses to give themselves up heartily to His service as the Redeemer of Mankind,—people who would shrink back disgusted from the ribaldry once current— are bewildered by finding what looks so like fairness and judicial impartiality united with open or thinly-veiled rejection of every thing most prominent in the ordinary conception of Him. They think they see a way by which they may still the long-felt craving of their hearts for a Saviour. And as men are never over eager to make the sacrifices involved in a true profession of the Christian faith, this new Gospel finds numerous adherents among those who, if they had had to choose between the two things which really are presented to them, the entire acceptance or total rejection of the Christ of the Gospels, would unquestionably have become Christians. As they fancy they are following the independent conclusions of their mind and conscience, they adopt this middle course, though the amount of credulity involved in such a plan is certainly considerably greater than that involved in the other. They must take their arguments ready-made from some one else. They are utterly unable to read the Bible in its original tongues. They have neither the time, the culture, nor the disposition to make a profound examination for themselves; and I think I am rather understating than overstating the truth when I assert that the blind deference paid to the utterances of leading writers on the side of unbelief is greater than that paid by the typical old woman of the Christian Church to her favorite preacher, at which they are never weary of directing the shafts of their raillery.

I have spoken so much at large on this point because I observe that many regard the commendation now so generally paid to our blessed Lord, even by those to whom He is only a good man, as something in all respects a matter for congratulation. I cannot think so. In some ways it is; and I have never doubted that it is a step toward true faith in Christ in some cases. But in the majority of instances, I am firmly persuaded that it is not so. The excuse it affords to one not much in earnest is very attractive. It frees him from the need of coming to a solemn resolve as to devoting his life to God or refusing to do so. Ignorant and blindly led as in the vast majority of cases such action most unquestionably is, it has nevertheless, what is to many minds a powerful fascination—

that, namely, of taking one's position apart from that of men ordinarily—

"Holding no form of creed,
But contemplating all."

And it is a growing tendency. I am as thankful to God as any man for the increasing earnestness which animates the Church, as well as other Christian bodies, in this country and in England particularly, but also throughout many parts of the world. I am not saying, observe, that the Church is not growing, and with unexampled rapidity, both in numbers and in zeal. What seems to me an unmistakable fact is that the influence of this powerful movement is diminished by the new attitude taken by the enemy—that many who would pass into the fold of Christ are stopped on their way, and many hindered even from setting out, by swallowing an opiate of the kind I have been describing. It does not necessarily produce the effects which some heated Christian writers would ascribe to it—that of ruining the moral character and leading on to immorality. Such assertions are as foolish as they are unjust. But so far as concerns what history shows to be the mightiest known agency in making men better and purer—so far as concerns their admission of Christ to the occupancy of their souls and the guidance of their lives, its influence is very wide-spread.

Now St. James is discussing a question so closely allied to this of which I speak, that I may appropriately enough apply what he says to the modern form of error. He is speaking to men who had passed through that stage in the religious career which consists in gaining a clearer view of a man's position towards God, and receiving the

first impulse toward living a Christian life—what we ordinarily term conversion. It is plain enough from the rebuke addressed to them, that they had not followed this
up to its natural consequences, but had so far relaxed
their efforts as to frame an utterly false notion of what
was their duty. They rested in that first stage or tried
to do so, forgetful of the truth that, like the water of baptism, grace, of which it is the outward and visible sign, is
corrupted by stagnation. He puts it to them then most
forcibly, that the influence of the divine impulse which had
been vouchsafed them was transitory in its nature unless
accompanied by earnest effort. That which must precede
any true Christian life—an understanding of their sinfulness, the hatefulness of sin, and the means appointed by
God for its forgiveness—all this was like a man's sight
of himself in a mirror. Unless repeated—unless made
habitual—it would fade away from the memory ; and all
the repentance, all the abhorrence of sin, all the self-surrender to the divine will and guidance, all the devotion to
the soul's true welfare, would die out, and give place to
that self-deception to which we so easily allow ourselves
to become subject.

He addressed himself to men who had distinct *consciousness* of their having been begotten anew by the word
of truth,—who had definitely taken the perfect law of
liberty as the rule of their life. But the grades of divine
influence are as manifold as the moral and intellectual endowments of men. One frequent device of our ghostly
enemy for keeping souls out of the reach of Christ's elevating, and purifying; and strengthening influence is, to persuade them that they must wait to profess themselves Christians until they have experienced some earthquake of the

soul that shall be as unmistakable as that which levels a
city to the ground. And it is only when we feel and
acknowledge that truth which St. James so beautifully
makes his own from some Greek poet*—only when we
gratefully accept the blessed teaching that *every* good gift
and *every* perfect gift is from above, and cometh down
from the Father of "heavenly and spiritual" luminaries,
with whom is no irregularity, or shadow, or change, or
eclipse—it is only then that we understand how benign
are His fatherly mercies, and how much more impartial is
the illumination vouchsafed the souls of mankind, than
the fickle and oft-eclipsed light of sun and moon by which
our earthly needs are supplied. No: wherever a holy
impulse is felt the Apostle teaches us to see the influence
of the divine Spirit. No matter how produced or how
resisted, it is His work. Whether immediately, as in those
very rare cases when men have been suddenly arrested by
resistless power, like St. Paul, or Gardiner, or Bunyan, or
in the far commoner way of teaching or private personal appeal, or yet again through the means of Christianity in its
softening and moulding influence on surrounding society
every where, we are taught that human nature, itself incapable of holy impulses, that is, impulses towards *God's*
personal service, is the conscious or unconscious subject of
mysterious and divine action.

If then, a truth so revealed, and so approving itself to
our humbler and more reverent self-inspection, be a truth
meant for application, the bidding of St. James remains applicable to all cases where one's religious nature is in any
way touched and attracted toward holiness, or personal

---

* πᾶσα δόσις ἀγαθὴ καὶ πᾶν δώρημα τελεῖον.

4

devotion to a personal God. In this wide conception of
the Holy Spirit's activity who can flatter himself on being
free from the solemn responsibility of hearing the direct
appeal from God: " Give me thine heart?" For, in one
way or in another, every one must have memories more or
less recent—more or less distinct—of times when the
serene joy of a life hid with Christ in God presented itself
to him as the one thing on which his heart might be se-
curely fixed among all the changes and chances of this
mortal world. You may habitually drown that still,
small voice, but the memory of having once heard it—that
is something you *cannot* drown. The bulwark of arguments against Christianity derived from knowledge or
from ignorance—from the lamentable defects of Christians
on the one hand, or on the other from the lofty demands
of Christianity, (or by a strange unreasonableness, from
both at the same time,)—all this defence on which you ordinarily rely so confidently, once proved no more substantial a barrier than the closed door where the Apostles were
assembled : Christ once passed silently and irresistibly
through them all, and found you behind your fancied de-
fences. He met you face to face, and claimed you as His
own child by virtue of His death to ransom you. It may
have been for only a moment : it may have been during
weeks and months. You may go your way, but you cannot wholly forget in heart, however it may be in your
life, what manner of meeting that was. And therefore I
claim you—Christ claims you—as one who knows what the
word is, of which, if you would not die, you must be a
doer, and not a hearer only.

Observe what the inspired apostle suggests as the
only explanation of this latter course on the part of

one who has thus *heard* the word of life. Commending itself, as where faithfully uttered it does, to man's conscience *in the sight of God*, the only way of getting any rest from its importunities, is to fancy one's self out of God's sight. I do not hesitate for one moment to admit that, in some cases, or, indeed, at some periods of Christian history, as a general rule, the religion of Jesus has been so presented as *not* to commend itself to any man's enlightened conscience, in the sight of God or out of it. When, for personal attachment *to* Christ, men substitute a mere set of barren dogmas *about* Him,—when the deepest yearnings and instincts of human nature are outraged by depicting Christ as justly suffering the real *wrath* of God the Father directed against His own sinless and obedient Son,—when Christianity is mixed up and adulterated with teaching that sin and its punishment may be bought off by fastings and vigils and hair-shirts and stripes,—under all these perversions there is presented something that revolts the manly reason ; and no wonder that this protest should find vent in rebellion and hostility.

Very much of the unbelief of a century ago in Europe was the direct and natural fruit of the disgust entertained by such courageous men as Voltaire for the organized corruption and tyranny that presented itself to him as the " *Holy* " Church. Much of what we find in our own day is to be laid at the Church's own door. In halting, worldly living—in narrow and fanatical bigotry—in unreasonable claims—in unfair argument—in blustering attempts to drown the voice of honest and sincere inquiry among God-fearing men really competent to make inquiry—in these and many other ways *some* have done an injury to

the cause of Christianity which can be repaired in no way
so well as by frank and sorrowful admission of all mistakes that have been made.   But while making such admission, I by no means admit that there is any excuse for
a man's adopting such an estimate of Christians generally.
It would be an admission which the facts do not justify to
say that any one need go far without finding plenty of
noble Christians, illustrating daily the doctrine of God
their Saviour in all things,—without finding good store of
men and books in whom " the sweet reasonableness" so
loudly urged by a most acrid and unreasonable writer of
the day is united with a deep and tender faith in all the
essential teaching of the Bible.   And it is because no fair
mind can dare for an instant to deny this that I hold the
apostle's words as true to-day as they were in the early
glow of Christian heroism : a man does " deceive himself"
if he pretends to be unable to see Christianity incarnated
in lives and in books of to-day.   He can hear the noblest
Christianity—he can see the noblest Christianity—he can
feel the noblest Christianity, by St. James' own definition
of pure religion and undefiled, if only he will look for it.
It is an influence which has produced our civilization.

The darkest periods of modern history are those in
which it has lost its hold on men; and therefore it is no
unreasoning prejudice to say that in all its true form it is
the world's hope and main-stay.   And so we come back to
the solemn charge of St. James: " Be ye doers of the
word, and not hearers only, deceiving your own selves."
There are many kinds of doing : belief is that which
must underlie all the rest.   Whatever may be your position then, whether nobly or feebly doing your duty within
the Church, or else sadly or with scorn refusing to do it

outside her pale, there comes this one command. We all need to heed it more. But the one thing which can make it what we need is to settle first of all our condition toward God. The sense of our human dependence upon Him—of our carnal frailty—of our unutterable obligations to Him who at such cost has redeemed us—this is what Christ only can tell us so that we can understand it.

In that grand sixth chapter of St. John's Gospel we have His way of communicating to men that priceless truth. He was asked what men should do that they might work the works of God. That is what every most earnest soul is asking now, as ever. And Christ's answer is plain: "This is the work of God, that ye *believe* on Him whom He hath sent." That, so far as one man can judge for others, is the answer which is most full of meaning, and which covers most ground for all who are eager in asking the first question. "Believe on Him whom He hath sent." All the divine nature, all the need of man for a Saviour, all that can change our life from a meaningless struggle for passing objects, seems to me to be contained in that reply. He whom God has sent is sent, rely upon it, on no needless mission. You need Him so mightily—so cravingly—so terribly, that that mighty need has brought Him down to meet it. Here you have Him—the incarnate love and tenderness and pitifulness of God's great mercy. He speaks to you—He pleads with you—He appeals to you not to deceive yourself with words that cannot profit. You have heard the word: do it. You have had Christ offered you: reject Him not. "This is the Father's will which hath sent me, that every one which seeth the Son and believeth on Him may have everlasting life; and I will raise him up at the last day." "Except ye eat the flesh of the Son of Man, and drink His blood, ye have no life in you." There, from the lips of Christ, are the promise and the warning. To you, and to you alone, is left the choice. Will you be a doer of the Word, or a hearer only, deceiving your own self?

VII.

ISRAEL'S DEMAND FOR A KING.

COMMUNION.

"And when ye saw that Nahash, the King of the children of Ammon, came against you, ye said unto me Nay, but a King shall reign over us : when the Lord your God was your King. Now therefore behold the King whom ye have chosen and whom ye have desired, and behold the Lord hath set a King over you."—1 SAM. xii. 12-13.

I THINK I am hardly mistaken when I suppose that for practical and devotional uses, a large part of the Old Testament has, in the minds of many excellent readers of the Bible, lost very much of its importance. With the exception of the Psalms, and certain portions of Isaiah, probably the instinctive feeling is that for one who has, or thinks he has, but little time for Scripture reading, the Old Testament is not to be compared in value with the New. And in a certain sense this general view has its measure of correctness; though even this is grossly exaggerated by our tendency to lose sight of one important fact. No doubt, supposing that we had to choose, which of the two constituent parts of our Bible we should retain, the choice involving the destruction of the other portion, there could be no hesitation in the mind of any one who had drunk in the meaning of the Saviour's life, who had experienced the salutary and invigorating effects of contemplating Christ's wondrous character, and who had found the central truth of his spiritual being to be conformity and intercourse with

79

the atoning Son of God. But no such choice lies necessarily before us, while still, with the exceptions just made,
the records of the secular dispensations have largely lost
their importance in our eyes. I will not attempt to investigate how much of this may be due to re-action from
the contrary mistake committed during, and before the
Commonwealth in England in the seventeenth century,
and by the Puritans in New England.

These two phases of religion, from which the rest of
Christendom, as well as the descendants of the Roundheads, have always gotten away as fast and as far as
possible, either on account of the bareness and uncompro-
mising simplicity of their theory of things, or on account
perhaps of the literalness at first of their conception of
moral duty. However much there may lie in this sugges-
tion to explain the fact, a good deal must be laid at the
door of the misconception at which I have hinted. That
misconception is, shortly, this,—an unconscious belief that
in other respects as well as in regard to our attitude towards the Old Testament, we stand in the same position as
the first generation of Christians immediately after their
conversion. On them no doubt, whether converts from
the Jews, or proselytes from heathenism, the New Testament possessed claims of so peculiar a character as almost
to call for exclusive devotion to the treasure of knowledge
for the first time disclosed in its records. The mind of
the Jew was already familiar with the story, and saturated
with the inferences drawn by many generations of com-
mentators from the text of the Old Testament. The pagan
convert was but freshly awakened to the existence of a
body of teaching whose simplicity of general outline, in
spite of some difficulty in detail, afforded a joyous con-

trast to the conflicting doubts and speculations of the philosophical schools, and whose transcendent purity shamed the gross polytheism of heathendom : hence, he must naturally have sprung to its study with an ardor which for a time could find room for no other pursuit. He had in the Gospels and Epistles, the truth to which the Old Testament had been mainly occupied in conducting, and he needed first to invigorate himself by assimilating the principles and facts of the New, before he could be in a position to understand the Old. For both Jews and heathens, however, this did not involve the abandonment of the revelation that had preceded.

The former, as we know from history, very soon came back to the position of ascribing an even unwarrantable authority to the law of Moses. And the writings of the earliest converts from heathenism show that they at once learned to look on the more ancient records as standing on a level with them; not, indeed, as possessing just the same value, but at least, as proved by the innumerable citations and constant use in the illustration and enforcement of Christian duty, in the light of an exhaustless storehouse of lessons in piety and practice.

With us, likewise, whom many generations of Christian forerunners have enriched with the inheritance of a firm belief in the New Testament, and a thorough sympathy with it, it is time that there should arise a juster estimate of the value of its hoary predecessor. We are *too much* inclined—I say this in spite of the wearisomely-iterated complaints to the contrary of many popular historians and essayists of to-day—we are *too much* inclined, in the Church at least, whatever may be the case with other religious bodies around us, to lose sight of the theological,

4 *

i. e. the scientific and dogmatic part of our religion. We
are too much disposed to think religion something which
may be wholly resolved into feeling, although the class of
writers to whom I refer are partly right in reproaching
Christians with so little doing, that feeling sometimes
grows sickly. That men in general, even when truly
religious, are top-heavy with an excessive knowledge of
theology, or absorbed by a too intense devotion to dogma,
to the history of the Church, or even to what is plainly
recorded between the covers of the Bible, appears to me
the most ridiculously groundless accusation ever urged.
Certain conceptions of particular spiritual processes have
unquestionably, in some cases, outgrown their proper
relative importance,—*e. g.* that of the office of faith, or
the Atonement even; yet I am not sure but that
the crying want of our times, quite as much as more *outward activity*, is a deeper study of the Bible, of Church
history, and a more intelligent faith in the doctrines
which necessarily shape themselves out of the statements
of Scripture. Why, the ignorance of the Bible is positively astonishing! The best educated of us are generally
far more familiar with the chronicles of Europe than with
those of Israel. Instead of studying sacred history, and
its divine principles, as we study the annals of England,
a large number of cultivated persons content themselves
with listening to the selected chapters which the Church
provides for Sunday morning, and have a painfully vague
and unconnected notion of the succession of events by
which our forerunners were educated as the champions of
monotheism. While, as for doctrine, depend upon it, one
whose profession has rendered necessary a study of it, is
often astounded at the ignorance displayed by men of cul-

ture, who venture flippantly to assail articles of faith, without the faintest glimmering of knowledge as to the severely logical processes by which (slowly and carefully aided by the labors of many councils and many generations), the instructed minds of the Church have been led to adopt them as the only secure standing-ground, against many plausible theories which would inevitably have developed errors tending to sap the very foundations of Christianity.

You think there is very little connection between all this and the text. I am brought to say it by my oft-repeated experience of the profound value of the Old Testament. To a mind which has drunk in the principles of the New, I think the Old presents, not only a great deal of light on the most important points in the relations of God to man,—that is what we call theology,—but an astonishing number of illustrations which serve as guides in daily life. Open it where you may, in the historic portions more particularly, you discover so close and singular a parallelism between the events there recorded and the spiritual history of the individual believer in Christ, that the feeblest imagination cannot fail to be impressed with the coincidence; and one understands how men should, in old times, have made use of it to solve their doubts by simply opening it at a venture, and taking the first verse on which the eye fell as an oracular utterance for guiding them out of their perplexity. Take, for example, the transaction recorded in this morning's first lesson. Listen to the hoary-headed Judge as he recounts the previous history of Israel, as he points out, through all their changeful past, the visible guidance of their invisible King, as he recalls to the minds of the assembled multitude their insane desire to sacrifice all the priceless advantages accruing to them from God's rulership, in order that they might have some human leader for the armies which once conquered all foes, in the simple might inspired by the conviction that it was the Lord who fought for them.

Listen to him, I say, and does there not rise up in your memory some vision of the counterpart to all this which you yourself have enacted? Do you not recall more than one crisis in which you abandoned the spiritual leadership which was educating you by its demand for a pure un-faltering faith that the things which are seen are temporal, and the things that are not seen are alone eternal? Look at those new rulers that you set up to rule over your-self,—that a guide belonging to earth might direct you in your earthly warfare, "when the Lord was" already "your King;" and even though the new ruler might tower over other men's motives, as Saul "was higher than any of the people from the shoulders and upward," see whether you have gained by the substitution. "Now therefore behold the king whom ye have chosen, and whom ye have desired, and behold, the Lord hath set a king over you."

I am not speaking now of those cases in which you may for a time have actually abandoned the great animating purpose of making your life a service to God. That would be a false parallel, and would resemble rather those cases where Israel gave itself up to idolatry, only to suffer from incursions of pitiless enemies, in ghastly likeness to caitiff souls who have deserted to the army of the devil. The resemblance in the present instance is rather to those periods, when, while acknowledging in general God's right to your fealty and obedience, you have grown dissatisfied with the pure spirituality of his rule, and demanded as the object for your closer and more immediate homage, something else, some high standard of duty, some definite and distinct mission, some special rule of life, which, by its iron enactments should obviate the dangers which, as you imagined, made the pure Theocracy unfit for a working plan. In order to be quite parallel with the period of Jewish history here dealt with, this desire on your part must have been one to which, in spite of its unfaithfulness to Himself, God could accede, one inspired by a sincere, though mistaken belief, in the greater efficacy of your own plan toward enabling you to do His will. This was partly the nature of the longing of Israel after a human monarchy. The longing was satisfied accordingly, not simply as a punishment, but as a means of educating them by the painful discipline of experience for a more hearty acceptance of the Theocracy as the best government for them. Have there been no such desires in our own lives, followed by a deeper conviction that the immediate rule of God was our safest and healthiest condition?

Take, for example, what is probably the experience of a large number of the highest and purest souls whom God takes into His great training school. The general view of the Christian life presented by the Bible, seems, to such souls brimming over with large and noble aspirations, a thing too vague for reduction to practice without some attempt at making it more precise in its character. Obedience toward God, yes surely, such a man will say to himself, that is a virtue which is the very foundation of all spirituality, and it alone causes the polar distance between such a life as is pleasing to Him, and the other life that is full of nobleness and earnestness, only deficient in that one transforming element. I can never commit the gross error of supposing two things such as those, so radically diverse, to be equally good. But why is this duty left so much to men's private judgment, weak, and deformed, and sinful as that so often is? Why are men not everywhere furnished with a more precise conception of what this great God is, whom we must love and adore? And so of the thousand other branches and varieties of human duty. Why are they left so indistinct and fluctuating that what to one generation is fit and proper, to another seems in violation of the fundamentals, not only of religion, but of morality?

If I have read off at all accurately the ponderings of many a God-fearing soul, then it is easy to see how precisely parallel they are with this phase of Israelitish story and its result. The oversight in both cases was the same. The chosen people of God evinced their distrust of Him and of His direct personal government of them, by insisting upon looking beyond the present into some distant future. They were chained down, like all human beings, to dealing in fact, with that which lay *immediately* before them. But this was not enough. The solemn oracles which, as occasion demanded, gave them the truth of God, the human instruments which, as it seemed to them chance, (in reality their divine Ruler) raised up, to free them from the oppressors, these were insufficient. They must have a human, visible King, like their neighbors, to lead them forth to battle.

Such precisely in kind, are the mistakes committed by souls of the class to which I am referring. First there is that assumption to which we are all so prone, that admitting all our past oversights *now* at last we are come to a point from which we may look onward, and form a reliable plan for future activity. We cannot trust the slow wisdom of God, which would enable us to act with sure conviction to-day, and leave to the growing insight begotten of the faithful discharge of to-day's task, the understanding of to-morrow's behest.

We look anxiously in our Bibles and are sorely disappointed at not finding there a clear definite scheme of duty regarding the new questions which our generation has to face, and to solve. We cannot believe that the divine Spirit who has directed us through the past, will suffice for the problem of to-day. Just so the Israelites were all split into warring, or indifferent factions when a new Gideon, or Samson, or Barak arose to the help of the Lord against the mighty, and demanded that this God-governed state of theirs, this yet fluid and molten mass out of which Jehovah was purposing to create a model for all the kingdoms of earth, should stiffen and harden into something just like what the nations around them were contented with. But is it not plain that we, in imitating them, are false to the divine purposes for us? We look around us, and are shamed very often by seeing in how trim and orderly a way some human lives are led who profess nothing but a stern sense of duty. Our shame is a very proper feeling, and can hardly be too deep. But surely it is too hasty an inference to draw, that all our uncertainties can be answered by abandoning the high hopes which make possible for us a grander future. This constant possession of a perfectly defined, clearly-seen object and a never doubtful method for reaching it, is shaped to meet the exigencies and the wants of earthly life, and them alone. It is not necessarily suited to all the aspirations of a life which is moved and swayed by eternal forces toward a goal eternally advancing. More shame for us indeed if with God's light to guide us, we do not distinctly make out just what our duty is *for the present*, and if with His arm to strengthen us we do not perform it. For these purposes we have, if we would only believe it, all we want.

But as the government of a great state, with its thousand points of contact with other nations, and its strong sense of a glorious future, is more embarrassing than that of some country village, so is it better to belong to one than to the other. You lead, I am supposing, a life that is genuinely pure and Christian, and your doubts and troubles arise from the lack of that placidity and evenness of tenor which you envy so in men that make no profession of being Christians. They experience none of the tumultuous swayings and tossings of soul with which you are familiar. Is not the reason simply this, that in all charity towards them, and with all condemnation of yourself, you must assume from their general demeanor that they do not aspire after God and His service, as you know men *can* do, but are content to live on a lower plane? The bare "duty" for which they are ready and able sometimes to make so noble sacrifices, is it, after all, worth your while to buy it at the cost of the Living God's dominion over you?

Magnificent and stern as is the symmetry of such a life, self-concentred, having reached the last point to which it can aspire, can you surrender, for its acquisition, those mysterious yearnings after rest in the bosom of God, those thrills of revelation from the unseen depths of eternity, those momentary glimpses of a life to which this is but the vestibule? Can you, I ask, surrender these, and admit to yourself that you have stopped at a point from which you shall never pass to climb the golden stairway that leads nearer and nearer to God forever?

You feel painfully that the Bible does not contain precise answers to the world's questions of to-day. Is it not clear that He could not, without destroying the Bible's *immediate* influence, have made plain to mankind at any one stage of their history all that one day He shall look for from them? The only thing that can be granted to all generations alike is the readiness to follow Him as he leads them upward along a path of which only a part can be disclosed distinctly to any single age, leaving its further windings up the mount of God to grow dimmer and fainter, until, at last, from our present standing-point, it fades away wholly amid the flaming glories of the throne.

Some vindication, I think, is becoming very necessary of the ways of God to man; some protest against the teaching which is growing very common that we may safely abandon theology, *i. e.* all that can be deduced from the Bible as to the relation in which we stand to Him, and content ourselves with putting on our soul's throne some regal form of duty apart from the direct *personal* rule of God.

The disputes to which theology has given rise have been many and bitter. The extent to which men have substituted a mental conception of divine truth, for an appropriation by the heart, has been lamentable; and in our day more dangerous, because presenting a more deceiving counterfeit of true Christianity. The cultivation of the religious tastes and feelings by all means, external and internal, has given too much cause for the summoning back of humanity to the mere unaided sense of duty. We have this subtle poison on every side. In all forms of literature from the most artistically perfect novel, or essay, or sober history, to the popular ballad, or the magazine sketch which decks out the revolting reckless-ness of life of frontier savages in the attire of a daring and superb self-sacrifice,—in all directions, we are presented with the thought that, provided only a man here and there does a noble thing he is serving God as acceptably as though the other three hundred and sixty-four days of the year were not besmirched with blasphemy and drunk-enness and lewdness. Are we prepared in the remotest sense, to adopt such a standard for ourselves, or to allow our charity for other men to pass into this extreme of laxity? Are we ready to admit that the mere fitful sense of duty is the last form of spiritual cultivation? Are we to forget, like the Israelites, all the triumphs that the Church has achieved with God at her head, because when she has lost her faith in Him she has been worsted? Are we like them, to demand a king that belongs to this earth, when the Lord our God is our King?

If we do, He will grant our prayer. We shall be made over to the dominion of just the ordinary motives which sway humanity, with only the doubly obscured conscious-ness that, from some far-off corner of the Heavens, He is watching us. I am much mistaken if the parallel will not carry itself out further than we dream, till after find-ing, like the Israelites, that our chosen protector cannot give us victory in the battle, we are brought back through some dreary Babylonish captivity to our old allegiance to God as the only ruler under whom our souls can grow. But I should not have said that in all things there is a parallel between God's ancient people and those of us who are tempted to put in the place of His guiding Spirit the earthly fidelity to mere duty apart from Him. They were more excusable than we. For as we assemble round the hallowed table to receive the elements which convey spiritual strength to the believing soul, are we not thrilled with a sense of shame at having even in thought wished to dethrone the man Christ Jesus in our hearts, and sacrifice to rules and principles, however pure and noble, His personal guidance? While Moses headed them, the Israelites never demanded any king but God. Here is Moses' antetype, He who may become the inmate of our hearts, stilling our impatient grasp after impossibilities, nerving the soul to achieve, in the sphere of present activity, ever braver feats of spiritual prowess. This the *divine* King can do, because, while He is very God, He is no cold, stern principle, stunting us into immobility in this our moral childhood, but a living, breathing, sympathizing man, full of loving tenderness, strengthening such as do stand, comforting and helping the weak-hearted, raising up those who fall, and animating us with the prospect of becoming daily purer, outgrowing all that we can now conceive of spiritual perfection, and so finally beating down Satan under our feet.

VIII.

SUNDAY AND ITS OBSERVANCE.

As the American, like the English and the Scotch Sunday is one of the most remarkable features of the national system, so Church-going in the countries named is a habit followed in a manner quite distinctive. I do not mean to say that as to both these matters there is not a good deal that is similar in certain parts of Germany and of Switzerland. But the general truth of what has been asserted can hardly be denied, namely, that Sunday is observed, and Church-going practised very differently here and on the Continent of Europe. A change however in respect to both, is beginning to force itself upon the attention. This is particularly the case in the great cities, where the infusion of a large mass of foreigners has tended to affect the native-born population, notably as to the opening on Sunday of places of innocent popular recreation, nowhere so much needed, perhaps, as by the laboring classes of our great sweltering cities in summer-time. The Sunday question has, in many localities, come to be a political question; and to those who know little of the results where the foreign population is large and united,—to those, for instance, who are familiar with the Sunday aspect of no great city but our own, it may seem that undue alarm has been conceived, and unduly harsh measures proposed or adopted, with the view of enforcing on all classes and nationalities, the Sabbath

92

views and practices hitherto prevailing among our respectable people. It is a very large question, and one hardly fit for treatment here, inasmuch as we have almost none of the complications to deal with on which I have touched. I believe, however, that we may find benefit from considering it so far as relates to ourselves. If the question be asked: What is Sunday, and how should we employ it, as decent members of society, and especially as Christians? the answer may tend to show that we are to some extent abusing our Christian liberty, and in some directions, perhaps, unduly restricting it. In what I shall say I do not doubt that I shall shock some who have most sternly held by the old Evangelical view, as well as seem narrow and Pharisaic to those who have most completely abandoned that view in both theory and practice. I should very much prefer to do neither,—to avoid the reputation of being lax, and the imputation of being narrow. And so, while I deplore the consequences that may result, I will ask you to listen patiently and fairly so far as you may.

Names are much more important as sign-posts indicating the course of thought and feeling than is generally supposed. And in the two common names applied to the first day of the week, we may find help in distinguishing more clearly the two differing sets of convictions prevailing in regard to the matter proposed for our consideration. The names by which that day is called are Sunday (prevailing generally in the Church), and Sabbath, whose use prevails so widely in the outside community, that when you write a notice for a paper, calling the day Sunday, you have to give special directions to adhere to copy, or you find yourself appearing to prefer the name Sabbath. The two words, as I have said, indicate the differing opinions held. Let us consider them, beginning with the latter.

As the name implies, those who use it regard the day as being essentially what the fourth commandment tells us the Sabbath was to be among the Jews,—a day in which no work should be done but that which is absolutely necessary to keep society from falling to pieces, or life from being lost. To this, however, has been added the duty of not doing anything but what has a distinctly religious character. This is the result of feeling that, as some occupation *must* be had, religious duties are those that the spirit of Christianity suggests as the only proper ones. This is the view that was general forty years ago among the classes that gave most outward evidence of being at all in earnest with their spiritual lives; and, though slowly changing with those who once held it most pertinaciously, it is still widely retained. Its ground is the truly noble and Christian one that the soul's interests are paramount in their claims to any others. Inasmuch as with a large proportion of mankind the week-days, as we call them, are filled with toil which can be made religious only by bringing into its discharge the sense of sonship and duty to God, this is almost the only time left for gaining religious knowledge, attending public service, and toning up our souls that they may the better resist the insidious assaults of the Evil One, to which they are sure to be exposed during the days that follow. I say that this temper of mind, this way of regarding the matter, is very pure, very high, very clearly revealing an earnest desire for spiritual growth. And as a matter of fact, the best Christians we know, whatever views they may hold about others and their duties, are in the habit of thus spending their Sundays, that is, in distinctly religious ways. One reveres this spirit instinctively, even when one cannot agree with the arguments by which the practice is sometimes supported. One of these arguments is the strict and unmistakable language of the fourth commandment. But in the first place, no attempt is made, that I am aware of, except in one insignificant Christian body, to observe the day there specified. No one tries to keep Saturday in this manner; and it is urged that the same authority that has changed the day may equally change the method of its observance.

Again, so far as the Jewish Sabbath was concerned, our Saviour Himself in deeds, and St. Paul in so many words, condemns the observance of the old Sabbath in the way which was then common, especially when it was looked upon as holy in itself—saying, that it was for each man to follow his own judgment, that is, in all probability, whether (as the Christian Church had not as yet regulated the matter) he should hold the seventh day, or any other day to be specially proper for religious observance. As to the manner of keeping the day; again, while the strictest obedience is never thought of, there is wide difference of view as to the extent to which it should or may be enforced on those under our authority as parents or employers. Some most conscientious and excellent people so change the day from one in which its character can be said to be that of rejoicing and being glad to any but the devoutest people, that a strong distaste for anything like religion is bred in the minds of children and servants. The attempt is sometimes made to shut out all but religious subjects from conversation, with results that are,

now and then, ludicrous enough. In short, as I have
said, occupations that, carried to this degree, are pleasing
to none but those who are far advanced in holiness are
enforced upon those whose natural restlessness, or whose
backward growth in religious things makes them regard
such control with bitter dislike, while other innocent occupations are sternly forbidden. The result in many and
many a case which has come under my own observation
is, that all that connects itself with religion is looked upon
so wrongly that with the first free step in life its restraints are cast off, and the reaction against enforced
piety brings about a melancholy plunge even into vice.

I do not pretend to have presented fully the arguments
that may be urged in defense of the Sabbatarian view;
nor is it meant, for an instant, that all households where
it is held present the extreme results spoken of. In many
cases where such abandonment of all moral constraint is
attributed to undue Sabbath strictness in childhood, this
may be fully matched by the disorders of one who has
been raised under a generous and wisely liberal system.
But as the reasons urged required consideration, mention
of practical results was unavoidable. Let me now turn
to a brief presentment of the other side.

According to this, the Jewish Sabbath, both in name
and nature has been abolished. To Christ's treatment of
the matter and St. Paul's I have already directed attention. As a duty to be enforced upon the members of the
Christian Church, we find absolutely no mention of it.
Instead, the first day of the week, both in the New Testament and in the earliest Christian writings which follow,
is spoken of as one of religious observance indeed, but of
a very different kind. It was a day for common worship,

but this was in weekly commemoration of Christ's rising again from the dead. It was as distinctly a new creation in its nature, as any of the other Church festivals, like its yearly analogue, Easter, or as Whitsunday; although, unlike them, dating back to the Apostles, and therefore having that superior obligation on us. It was a day of happy Christian enjoyment—that is of enjoyment primarily religious. And such, observe, it continued to be until after the Reformation. The great continental Reformers, Luther even, and Calvin, had no more notion of enforcing the Puritanic Sabbath than of rebuilding the Temple at Jerusalem. As we find it referred to in the New Testament as the first day of the week, as the Lord's Day, so its character there is that of a stated time for religious meeting, for worship, for alms-giving, for celebrating the Holy Communion, for exhortation and instruction. As such for fifteen hundred years it was observed, and not until the times of the English and Scotch fanatics was it ever regarded as a day when all that was not directly religious should be forbidden to all, of every age, of every condition, of every degree of mental and spiritual advance. We are in accord, not in disagreement, with the whole of the Church's previous history, when we deny that this last view of Sunday's proper enjoyment is binding upon us.

But what follows from all this, incontestably true though it be? Does it follow that, either as members of a Christian community, or as living members ourselves of the body of Christ, we are at liberty to follow our own devices on the Lord's day, and to amuse ourselves just as we should on the fourth of July, to spend its hours in the lax ways so common? In general, certainly few of us are prepared

5

to assume so much as that. In drawing the line lies the difficulty; and it is just here that I want you to take what I say only as a hint toward the proper solution of the problem, not as meant to point out as wrong-doers and profaners of the day all who do not agree with it.

As the first principle to guide us, we must remember the needs of our souls, and the difficulties most of us have, or make, about satisfying them. In regard to public worship in general, it would be cruelly unjust to set down the business man or the laborer as indifferent, because he did not see his way clear to leave his daily calling to attend service on all the holy days when it is offered him. So in regard to spiritual exercises generally; the man who must be at his plough, or his desk, early every morning, is, of necessity, debarred from devoting as much time to prayer or to reading as others may give. But, unless the position is taken that these things are needless, it would certainly seem to follow that, where any earnestness is found, there would be a duty and also a disposition to use some of these quiet hours in training himself to better knowledge and deeper thought. It is not that this one day should present an utterly different aspect from all the rest of his life, but that in proportion as all the rest of his life is genuinely swayed by spiritual motives, the day when he is at liberty to gratify his deepest desires would be increasingly devoted to such pursuits. But, you will say, suppose him not to be in just the mood you speak of,—suppose him to be on the level of the great body of even Christians, and not so ardent about these things, how shall he pass this day, which comes round weekly, and which he *must* pass in some way, and which leaves him tired and in anything but a charitable or happy frame of mind, when he does nothing but what is sometimes recommended? That is just the difficult question to answer, because the reply, however guarded, is sure to be wrested by some, and used in justification of what they themselves know to be wrong. I would rather give it in private than in public; but as almost no one will ask it but those who are a little *over*-scrupulous already, some attempt must be made in public. It is the question of one who practically refuses to do what would remove the difficulty, and asks how far he may allow his unfitness to act as a plea for not doing all his duty. I propose to give only a few suggestions, which will approve themselves to your judgment only in so far as you may agree with what I have already said. But I am often struck with the fact that persons by no means remarkable for strictness in their general demeanor, have a decided feeling about the observance of Sunday, and need only a reminder to arouse them to a more proper manner of keeping the day. To speak first of what should *not* be done. If the day is to have anything of a religious character, the reading one does should certainly be to a large extent of that kind. This may seem a very gloomy piece of advice, even to many who call themselves Christians. And nothing surprises one more than the extent to which the reading of religious books is neglected, even by those who have some considerable degree of culture. The number of books of really fascinating interest upon such subjects is very great; with all the charms of deep scholarship, of glowing fancy, of keen logic, of limpid style they come to us, especially from England, with attractions far greater than are presented by a large proportion of the works on secular subjects, which are devoured so eagerly. Yet they are not read to anything approaching the extent one would expect, even among persons who profess an interest in the subjects of which they treat. At all events this is the case among the upper classes so far as position and refinement go, while those immediately below them in these respects differ very markedly. If you want to know more about sacred subjects, however, you certainly cannot complain of a dearth of literature, and very charming literature, to meet your wants.

Another thing which certainly is hardly in keeping with the sacred character of the day is following the same amusements as serve for relaxation during the remainder of the week. Very few of those who amuse themselves with cards would think of spending Sunday afternoon at such games, and yet the day is sometimes spent in amusements which, while innocent enough in themselves, are certainly quite foreign to the mood which sees in Sunday a day primarily intended to elevate and dignify our nature, and fit us for a closer walk with God. To one who deliberately denies this position, of course there is nothing to be said on that point. But another argument remains which has sometimes proved of weight with those who had some regard for their fellow-men. The day, as I have said, is a national institution. We know what it is on the Continent of Europe; and few of us, I imagine, desire to see the day degenerate here into what it is, for instance, in France or in Spain, where great public displays, horse-races, elections and the like are habitually held upon it. But the change to such a view is vastly helped by observing that men of leisure and influence in the community pay little or no attention to its sacred character. The refined enjoyments in which you choose to pass your Sunday are out of the reach of most of those around you. If they learn from your example to desecrate it, as learn they surely will, sooner or later, it will be done in a very different manner; in brutal sports such as must debase the national character. You may not enjoy the day so keenly if you place some restraints on your liberty in the matter; but the knowledge that you are harming others as well as yourself by treating it with such scant respect,—the feeling that you are contributing powerfully to destroy the institution which has been so useful to our race,—to break down one more bulwark erected against the inroads of irreligion,—these reflections, one would think, would have great weight with one who honestly loves his country.

I have made one or two suggestions—I meant to do nothing more—which if attended to would, I am sure, redound to the benefit of all. Let me now say a few words about church-going and certain obvious duties connected with it. The uses of church-going are plain. One *might*, it is true, learn as much, so far as facts go, by staying at home and reading the service and a sermon; but he would miss the very thing for whose sake we are bidden not to forsake the assembling of ourselves together,—I mean the curiously different way in which one is impressed, when one of a number, from that in which one feels when alone. Reason about it as we may, and extol as we may the advantages of reading over hearing, it remains true that worship in common supplies us with something that would not be afforded by reading at home, even were that practised, as it seldom is, by those who willingly absent themselves from the House of God. The prayers are fuller of devotion, the Bible more replete with meaning, the teach-

ing impresses more deeply, on just the same principle as
that which draws people to listen to a famous lecturer,
even though his delivery be mediocre, in preference to
reading one of his essays at home.   But over and above
this, we come, or should come to church, with a feeling
that it is, in a very true and deep sense, the House of God.
We come to confess our sins, to be assured of forgiveness,
to pray for the divine blessing.   We *expect* a benefit from
the observance.   Such is the state of mind which alone
befits those who attend church.   What is one to think of
the frames of mind of such as choose habitually to come
so late as to disturb the devotions of others, or who are
perpetually whispering or gazing around, when there, as
they would in a play-house?   Where lateness is actually
unavoidable, and not due to Sunday-morning laziness, it
is another thing.   But those who will reflect how excess-
ively disturbing it is to people who want to attend to their
religious duties, to have the constant interruptions, and the
still more annoying whispers,—such persons will see the
propriety of making an effort to be punctual at church,
and of behaving themselves with decorum when there.

Many churches, at the present day, are free,—hence,
having no pew-rents, they depend altogether upon volun-
tary contributions.   Let those who attend such a church
come with the intention of contributing to its support as
liberally as their means will allow, and not of putting into
the plate some insignificant coin which they are half-
ashamed to have seen.   Giving is as much, and as necessary a part of worship, as prayer.

I have used considerable plainness of speech.   Where
a thing has to be said perhaps it is as well to say it so
that it may be understood, and on that principle I have

spoken. For the matter is one of no mean importance. Upon the proper observance of Sunday and its duties, hinges to a very large degree the spiritual life of most of us. That is to say, where Sunday is habitually spent in a careless and non-religious way, there you may certainly look to see the family growing up in anything but the way a Christian parent could wish. It is of the highest importance to ourselves, to the community, nay to the nation and the world at large which we must increasingly influence, that this time-honored, this sacred institution shall retain the share it has hitherto had in moulding the American character.

It becomes growingly clear, even to those who make no profession themselves, that in Christianity lies the mainstay of a nation's existence. The wild visionaries who dream of putting into execution the crazy plant of communism, show us with perfect distinctness the point whither natural greed, uncurbed by morals or religion, must always tend. And, whatever may be our private theories or practice, nothing can blind an unprejudiced eye to these two facts : the first is that every man's desecration of the day leads to its violation by others : the second is that where Sunday is decently observed, there you find peaceable, law-abiding, and respectable people. I look then upon the institution as one of the utmost importance ; and I urge you for the sake of your souls, for the sake of family and country, to observe it piously, reverently, as becomes a day which is set apart from all others with the distinctive title of the Lord's Day. In so far as this is done will our homes be more and more the abodes of earnest, manly piety, and such serene peace as ever falls to his lot who putteth his trust in the Lord and doeth good.

IX.

ALL SAINTS.

"That they without us should not be made perfect." —HEB. xi. 40.

IN all ages of humanity, it is likely, the craving has been felt to hold communion with the dead. It is hard to feel that he who was yesterday among us, sharing our joys and sorrows, limited by our imperfections, and as unable as we to penetrate the mystery of being, should have suddenly shot ahead by all the distance separating life on earth from life in Paradise. Not that at first we envy him the flood of light which, we are sure, illuminates for him the whole range of spiritual truth; so far as that is concerned, we are tempted, in spite of our conviction that with the Lord he is far better, to *feel* about him as though he were still in the condition of weakness in which he took his departure. But when we rid ourselves of this feeling and learn to think of him as among the joys of Paradise, drinking in the unending stream of knowledge and love, we are penetrated by the cruel pang of feeling that we are left so far behind that we must be forgotten,—that all memories of earthly communion must be swallowed up in the new emotions aroused by a change so total of environment and association. This, to a truly loving heart, must be one of the keenest pangs in losing a life-long companion; and it is not every one who can, like Tennyson, wrestle with his doubts, and work out the con-

104

viction that Love is Lord of all—Lord even of a change like this.

Then again, we want to know more of what actually lies beyond the tomb—what the departed are experiencing now, and what is in store for ourselves when our summons shall have come. And once more, in those many cases where, while on earth, the divine life has manifested itself imperfectly and fitfully,—where, but for our faith in God's promise of certainly granting whatever is unitedly asked by two or three of His faithful servants, we might doubt as to the reality of a friend's salvation,—in those cases where our faith is unwavering that prayer has been answered, but where we know that our dead must have entered Paradise very imperfectly developed by earthly discipline, and needing just those graces which, were they on earth, we should implore for them—in cases like these, the disposition to accompany them, even in their ransomed state sublime, with our tender solicitude and prayers, is one which is inexpressibly powerful.

These, and such as these, are feelings that spring from the lowest depths of our mysterious nature. And it is not to be wondered at that under their influence, beliefs should slowly have grown up, and practices have been gradually introduced, intended to satisfy these inextinguishable yearnings. The feeling, for instance, that our prayers may, without presumption, be put up for those who are departed in the communion of the Catholic Church, and, as we believe, in the confidence, however feeble, of a reasonable, religious, and holy hope,—this very early took shape; and in the age immediately following the Apostles, I find in the strange book known as the Shepherd of Hermas, traces of such a practice. In the Roman branch

of the Church, as every one knows, this doctrine has connected itself with the equally unscriptural doctrine of
Purgatory; and prayers for the dead are as commonly
offered as prayers for the living. Our own branch of the
Church, however, has not admitted either of these views
since the Reformation, and no one can plead for belief in
them, anything contained in her formularies. The doctrine of Purgatory, at least, is distinctly condemned.

Compared with what has arisen from the other sources·
I have named, the practice of praying for the dead is, to
say the least, much less harmful. That is wholly unwar-
ranted either by the Bible or our Church, and its practical consequences show it to be very full of danger. But
those systems of belief which spring from a determination
to *know* more than has been revealed of the condition of
the soul after death, such as Spiritualism and Swedenbor-
gianism, are degrading and materializing in the highest
degree. All that to a spiritual mind is purest and most
elevating in what we are told concerning our future life is,
in these systems, dragged down and bemired in such a
way as to make one feel that, if this is all that is in store
for us, annihilation would be far preferable to such disappointment of our loftiest aspirations.

But the Church of God has not contented itself with
condemning the doctrine of Purgatory, and omitting from
her system the practice of prayers for the dead, as well as
all rash attempts that have been made to penetrate the
veil hanging between our present and our future state.
Such a merely negative position would ill accord with her
duty as the teacher, through human agencies, of *all* that
God has intrusted to her. Pondering over the glimpses
afforded in the Bible into our future destiny, she has gath-

ered thence all that sound criticism permits us to infer on this subject, and has formulated it partly in her creed, and partly in certain of her prayers. She has, moreover, according to her wont, not allowed these truths to run the risk of the neglect to which mere words are liable. She has given them shape by admitting among the festivals of the Church year, the memory of certain of the primitive heroes of the faith of whom we have clear knowledge from the Bible; excluding, in the American branch at least, all those about whose history hangs the thick veil of mere tradition. And in the festival which we celebrate to-day, she yearly summons us to commemorate *all* those, known by name or unknown, who, having finished their course in faith, do now rest from their labors.

An article of the Apostles' Creed teaches us to believe in the Holy Catholic Church as being not confined to those who at any period of the world's history are fighting the Lord's battle *on earth,* but as being composed of all Saints, both those living, and those who are now at rest in Paradise. Nor is this all. The expression used to convey this grand conception of the Church suggests, or rather, most distinctly declares, not only that all these are *one,* but that there exists among all, irrespectively of any separation caused by death, a Communion; so that we do not in the Creed make two articles out of these two thoughts, but profess a belief in the Holy Catholic Church as *itself* being the Communion of Saints. The Church *is,* under one most true aspect, such a communion.

But you may say, is this all? This craving to know more of the mysteries of the future state—future to us but present to the faithful departed—this yearning by our prayers to help them on as we used to help them when they were with us—this desire that we should not be deprived of their intercession now that they have passed beyond the stage of discipline and are so much better able to pray for us than when earthly hinderances made their supplications less fervent and, so, less efficacious—is there nothing to answer all these deep-seated longings more than the assurance that there exists a vague communion between us and them?

I feel in all its force the yearning that gives birth to questions like these even though they are not often distinctly asked. And because I appreciate it, and am, at the same time, convinced, that there is danger and presumption in pressing beyond what the Bible tells and the Church proclaims on this matter, I propose to-day to point out how much there is in this article of the Communion of Saints, as our Church teaches it, to meet every legitimate demand.

In the first place, as to the state of the faithful departed. A notion prevails among some Christian bodies that the faithful are at once admitted after death to heaven— meaning by that word the full state of perfected bliss. Such a view makes of the Last Judgment, so far as their condition is concerned, a mere formality. It is, moreover, very hard to reconcile with the Biblical words employed in making the few distinct statements vouchsafed on the condition of the soul before the Judgment. Thus, for instance, our Saviour said to the penitent robber that he should be *with Him that day* in Paradise. But we know that our Lord did not, either on that day nor for many days afterward, ascend into heaven; for He distinctly told His disciples so. We know likewise, that during the period between His death and His resurrection He went and preached unto the spirits in prison—that He descended into the lower parts of the earth, as St. Peter and St. Paul assure us. That state or place then, that is called Paradise, or Hades (that is the invisible), was a place or state in which were the spirits of the dead, and to it, along with Christ, went the soul of the robber. But, though spoken of as a prison, so far as the wicked are concerned, it is nevertheless spoken of at other times when the spirits and souls of the righteous are treated of, as a place or state of bliss, to which such a man as St. Paul looked forward with eager yearning, as one whose delights in the presence of the Lord were so powerfully attractive, that much effort was needful if he would bear contentedly the burden of daily duty and the care of all the Churches. The word used in the original is totally different from those employed concerning the state of final bliss or that of final woe. Its derivation and meaning imply that it is mysterious, but not that it is other than full of joy to faithful souls.

We are, further, led to the same conclusion (viz., that Hades, or the place of departed spirits is different both from hell and from heaven) by reflecting on the very emphatic way in which we are told, in the first place that the soul will not be rejoined with the body until the final resurrection, in the second, that flesh and blood cannot enter into the kingdom of heaven, and in the third, that the last stage of God's dispensations (that is the entrance of human souls into the kingdom of heaven) will not begin until this corruptible shall have put on incorruption— which in St. Paul's grand chapter to the Corinthians, evidently means: until we shall have been reunited with our spiritual body. If entrance to heaven (in the full and proper sense of that word) is possible only after the resurrection, and the resurrection is not to take place until about the time of the Last Judgment, it would seem to need no further proof that, as our Lord said, no man hath ascended up into heaven as yet.

And yet again, we are established in such a belief by considering the marvellous influence over the mind by the body, and the intimate connection between them. We have no experience of a disembodied state, and therefore are totally without any conception of what such a state may be. But there is certainly reason to suppose that God would not so carefully assure us of the immortal destiny of the body—that Christ would not be distinctly called the Saviour of the body—that the reuniting of the soul to the body would not be made a *necessary preliminary* to entrance upon the state of perfected bliss—it is, I say, reasonable to suppose that God would not have assured us of all these things were there no peculiar fitness in the union between soul and body to enhance our highest interests. And if so, however happy may be the intermediate and disembodied state of the righteous, however fully the capacities of such a condition may be satisfied—still in the words of the text, they cannot be made perfect without us—they have still in anticipation a state of being into which they are not to enter until we,—all the faithful who dwell on earth—shall have joined them, and until, the present dispensation over, the new era shall have been inaugurated by the general resurrection.

It is hardly necessary to say that this view has no connection with the unscriptural doctrine of Purgatory. Purgatory is the purging or cleansing place. According to the Romish view, the wicked who are not finally to enter heaven do not go to Purgatory. But all those who have, at death, any remains of sin, go thither to be purged by further suffering of those remains of sin. It is, then, a continuation of pain, though not of probation; for all those who enter there are sure of ultimate bliss, though it may be long before all their sinfulness is refined away. There may be comfort in the thought to those who believe it,—there may be, and I have no doubt there is, a profound satisfaction to pure and loving hearts, in the belief, which of course is closely connected with it (though not with our Church's doctrine of the intermediate state), that by prayers, and alms, and good deeds, they may shorten the time of trial to which their dead are otherwise destined. I can see all the beauty and attractiveness of such a belief, which allows room for the intense yearning of the bereaved still to sacrifice for the departed the life-blood that was so willingly poured out for them on earth. But it is to be observed that there is no real advantage in it beyond that of our own scriptural teaching, as regards any greater room for hope concerning the departed. It still leaves the same sharp line of demarcation between those who are to be ultimately saved and those who are finally condemned. Wherever a Romanist has ground for hoping that the fitful manifestations of religious feeling on earth give assurance that a friend has been admitted to purgatory, where he is safe, however long may be his purgation,—in all such cases we have precisely the same ground of hope that the departed soul has been admitted to a state where, in the presence of God, and surrounded by none but elevating influences, he may grow into the measure of the stature of the fulness of Christ. And the advantages being the same,—the opportunities for exercising faith and hope being identical—both leave, as they must leave forever undetermined in this life, where the line is drawn which divides hope from despair,—both are compelled in the exercise of the highest spiritual self-surrender, to leave the determination of that point to the absolute justice and infinite mercy of our Father in heaven.

As American churchmen, then—as men who find in mere vague tradition no reasonable ground for belief—we are to think of our departed only as we are warranted by the word of God. They are not in heaven, since that fulness of perfected bliss is reserved until we shall have joined them, and can enter it with them. They are happy in the presence of the Lord, having the same spiritual privileges as we on earth ; only that they are adapted, and probably enlarged, as befits their freedom from temptation, and their confidence in an assured eternity of bliss. If their religious life on earth was weak, no doubt they pass into that state with less power of drinking in the fulness of joy than if their natures had taken kindly to discipline and trial here. The dying robber just opening his new-born eyes to the truth as it is in Jesus, can hardly be supposed to have entered at once upon the spiritual glories to which he was so suddenly admitted, with the same powers and capacities as those which St. Paul and St. John carried with them to Paradise. But all, no doubt, according to the measure of the gift of Christ,—new-born children and long-tried heroes of the faith,—experience an ever-increasing enlargement of their faculties, and love, believe, and hope more and more perfectly and fully until the last day.

Some such statement of the Church's reading of Bible-doctrine was needful, partly for itself, and, because all do not possess it in its wholeness, partly as a preparation for understanding fully the doctrine of the Church's being the Communion of Saints. In such a condition as, *we must suppose from the declarations of the Bible,* theirs to be, enjoying the presence of Christ, how can we help believing that we are the objects of their thoughts—that the course of the world, and particularly that of the Church is deeply interesting to them? Even if we do not undertake to decide whether they are permitted themselves to watch the ongoing of our lives, still they must receive all that is needful for being fully cognizant of our fortunes from the never-ending stream of messengers whom we are sending from our firesides to join their company. All that most interested them here must take on a new, and more vivid attractiveness when their eyes, from straining to detect the traces of God's ways on earth, and strengthened by the trial, gaze undimmed upon the Lord God of all the heavenly hosts. The growth in every Christian grace which seems inseparable from such a condition, must surely invest all pure, earthly affections with fresh strength. They must long and pray for the speedy accomplishment of God's purposes in general, and in particular for the perfecting of all whom they have left behind. That we should pray *for* them, is not only unauthorized by our Church, but apparently superfluous: that we should pray *to* them is to forget that we have no reason to suppose that they can hear our prayers. But that there is among them real communion in spirit with ourselves, the same spiritual nourishment and support vouchsafed to both parts of the Church, the militant and triumphant—the keenest interest with them, in both the general and particular providence of God, as far as knowledge is communicated to them either by God, or by those who are perpetually added to their number from earth ;—of this I cannot doubt without supposing them to be in a state of unconsciousness quite impossible to reconcile with what we are told ; and I no more doubt it than I doubt of the communion existing between the Church in England and the Church in America.

But communion is between two. Allowing that some such knowledge of and interest in us exists among the saints in Paradise, real communion demands that we too, should feel deeply and constantly that the tie uniting us to them is real. And I think it can hardly be gainsaid that when the mother Church in England rejected the doctrine of Purgatory, and the practice of Invocation of Saints, many of her children, forgetful of the wise caution with which she preserved the truth, while casting aside the perversion of it, came to feel an unreasonable aversion to the very mention of saints, as though their memory could not be cherished, nor their communion with ourselves maintained, without falling into the practices and the beliefs of the Church of Rome. If such practices and beliefs were necessarily connected with the doctrine set forth by our Church, that would be the most convincing proof that we ought never to have condemned them. For this doctrine may, in the words of the Article, be read in Holy Scripture and proved thereby ; and whatever necessarily follows from the true doctrine must itself be true. But the true belief and the innocent practice may be held by individuals, and taught by the Prayer Book, without such consequences. And we deliberately forego much that will tend to the sweetening and enlarging of our religious lives, if we permit this great truth to remain without its proper influence.

Who does not see and rejoice over the quickening of the interest felt by our own communion in the old Catholics, and the Holy Eastern Church? In both cases there may be differences which only time can wholly remove: such in the latter case certainly exist. But the longing desire that the unity of the Spirit should take outward shape is beyond question a feeling directly inspired by a larger, more vigorous Christian life. And, if we may anticipate the time when it shall have been realized,—if we may joyfully look forward to a period, however remote, when the mis-understandings of the past shall have been removed---when additions to the faith shall have been pruned away—when all branches of the Church shall be united in deed and in truth, and the whole of Christ's dispersed sheep shall have been gathered into the one fold—why shall we not now, try to realize more habitually the sublime truth that a host of saints infinitely outnumbering all who now believe on earth, are one with us in feeling, in thought, in aspira-tion, as they tread the happy walks of Paradise? There is nothing to hinder it but our undue absorption in the present and the visible. The great French statesman who died not long ago, left in his last will the solemn record of his conviction, that in the eternal light which he was about to enter many of the discussions which distract us here would appear to have arisen from our incapacity fully to take in the proportions of divine truth. No doubt they will, and no doubt our perfect union with other branches of the Church *militant* may long be delayed. But our union with the Church triumphant no man can hinder. That is beyond peradventure. Only strive to take it in,—only try to picture to yourself that multitude that no man can number, chanting ceaselessly the song which we

on earth are singing—strain your ear to catch the music of
that resounding symphony—and the true Church will
swell to proportions more majestic and inspiring—your
Christian life will recognize the proper sweep of its sym-
pathies—the hallowed feast in which we are about to join
will become, more particularly on this festival of All
Saints, the sublimest, as well as the deepest expression of
the truth that the Holy Catholic Church is the Communion
of Saints, no less with each other than with their ascended
Master.

X.

ST. MATTHEW.

THE VALUE OF THE OBSERVANCE OF SAINTS' DAYS.

THE celebration of the Saints' days is a feature of the Church's system which is gradually attracting more attention than formerly, but about which a good deal remains to be said. One need not be very old to recall the time when this, and many other practices which are distinctly enjoined in the Prayer Book, were by almost universal consent ignored. In some dioceses and parishes, the observance of them is still held, apparently, to be out of keeping with true Evangelical principles. The observance, by public worship at least, of the Ember seasons, the use of the prayers for those about to be ordained, holding ordinations at those times when they are specially ordered by our Canon, *i. e.*, immediately after the Ember weeks, the keeping of Saints' days,—these, or most of these, are matters which, in this country at least, have become general only within the memory of persons still in middle life. But although such Churchly observances are not, at the present day, likely to attract much thought from their novelty, the number of persons who give much attention to them is still very inconsiderable. Many who would be much annoyed at the thought of having public service given up on days appointed for it—who would, and rightly, consider the Church system neglected by such an omission,—are still by no means inclined themselves, to pay any tribute

117

of personal respect to these same matters. Such being
the case, one wonders how deep is the reverence for the
Church on the part of persons of this class. The thing is
a little strange, (is it not?) that what is ostensibly held so
important for a clergyman to attend to, should be left so
largely in his hands alone. It might be thought that
when the Church is opened for morning prayers, on days
specially apppointed for them, on days which have been
observed for many centuries by all branches of the Catholic
Church as commemorating the Saints of old, our forerunners in the faith, more than a handful of worshippers
would assemble in a parish where Church principles are
held important, and where there is a considerable number
of persons who are not too closely occupied to spare half
an hour for showing their principles to be based on conviction.

Let us view this matter somewhat carefully, and see
whether the Church has not displayed in this particular,
that same wisdom which has characterized her in other
matters.

In the great struggle for good against evil, various
methods have been tried for the purpose of bringing home
to men the great truths of morality and religion. One
system, which seems never to lose its charm for a certain
class of minds, is that of putting these truths into proverbs
and maxims,—a shape so compact and portable that the
mind may easily be stored with a large provision of rules
ready to be applied in time of need. On all planes of moral
and religious truth this system has been applied. You
have on the lowest plane, maxims of the worldly and selfish kind, which are calculated to keep one on the broad
highway of honesty, thrift and economy. In a higher

sphere you may find in abundance short, wise sayings of great thinkers, which contain the quintessence of long and patient thought applied to the loftiest subjects of human reflection. The Bible contains a book which shows that the divine mind has not omitted this in its multiform provisions for the needs of man, and whatever may be done in the way of condensing for practical purposes the lessons God would teach us, may be found in that wise and witty collection of old Hebrew maxims, with its introduction of sublime and generous eloquence, that robs the proverbs of all the mere worldliness that might otherwise be imputed to them, and shows the temper of religious reverence in which they are to be carried into effect in every-day life.

Another method of elevating men, and inducing them to lead a purer life, is to be found in the great systems of philosophy and morals which have been constructed in all ages, and in such profusion that our only difficulty is to choose among them. Here the claim is a little more substantial than when mere maxims are credited with much influence over the human mind. A somewhat more accurate view of our real needs prompts this attempt. For here the endeavor is made by giving something like a consistent general view of the moral universe, to supply what the better kind of men crave as the basis of their action. They never can be greatly influenced by mere proverbs, throwing at best only gleams as from a dark-lantern, upon this or that particular deed, or doubt, or desire. They may, perhaps, be roused to strive after a higher life, by having placed before them a system which will show them what are the objects after which they should strive— what are the means of giving efficacy to their strivings—

what the support, and what the incentive to sustain and inspirit them, when novelty is gone and the weariness and unprofitableness of human life weigh them down.   This is what alone has reaped any measure of success among the numerous efforts of philosophers and philanthropists.   Men *must* have some explanation, true or false, of the source and object of human existence, of its solemn facts of woe and wrong, to uphold them in any continuous efforts to lead a life higher than that of the mere seeker after pleasure, and shield them from the temptation which presents itself so often to us all, to say, in one shape or another, "Let us eat and drink for to-morrow we die."

And yet here also a mistake lies at the root.   Frame your system of philosophy, or of morals, with all the skill of which you are master—infuse into it all the warmth and enthusiasm of which it is capable—present it with whatever zeal you may—show as clearly as possible that it explains the problems of life;—and still you have done but little to ensure it any measure of success.   For the student in his library, it may be perfectly consistent with itself, and with the world for which it proposes a solution. But its power stops short when it passes from the study, the abode of thought and meditation, into the world of action and temptation.   It has little ability to make men hear the voice which spoke there so clearly and persuasively, when they are beset behind and before by the covetous desires and inordinate love of riches of which we hear in the collect for St. Matthew's day.   And more than this.   The proportion of mankind with whom even the idea of acting in accordance with it can find an entrance is exceedingly small.   Those who have a natural turn for thought and investigation may find time to study and be convinced. But for that immense portion of our race who have neither the time nor the capacity for reflecting over any such system,—who would not shape in words the difficulties, nor the cravings of which they are, nevertheless, deeply conscious,—for them, any explanation, or any scheme of life of this kind is absolutely ineffectual, even to command their assent.

The only way of really influencing men at large is by example. It is a power which we see and feel at work every day—every hour of our lives. It is always at work, always busy, even when we are not conscious of what is going on. How *good* it is in circumstances which give it a beneficent turn, we see in what looks like the *magic* of every wise and good family circle, community, nation. How *destructive* it may be, appears from the almost hope - less character of the attempt to do good to one who is sur- rounded by crime during the years of childhood and youth. Who of us do not know the subtle way in which it works when we get away from the ordinary constraints of home among those whom we see throwing off the bur- den of duty and self-respect? How it steals into the mind, persuasively suggesting the harmlessness and plea- sure of going and doing likewise! We say "No," and think we are very firm in our hold upon our common rules. But unless we are on our guard most jealously we find ourselves curiously advancing a little nearer, only to examine for ourselves, of course, and then, suddenly, overpowered.

This power of example is one of which Christianity makes the largest use; and it is, of all the principles of human nature, that which is most wisely and effectually employed. Many of the most striking of the *words* of

6

Christ are only in another form what had been said before Him. He based His teaching largely on the previous revelation. The duty of loving our neighbor as ourself, He advanced, not as a truth hitherto unknown, but as summing up and underlying the Law and the Prophets; while loving the Lord our God, with all our heart, and mind, and soul, and strength, was continually advanced in the Scriptures of the older dispensation. What was entirely new was the personal power with which He clothed those grand and simple truths. The Pharisees had at their finger's end all the minutest prescriptions of the Law, and had developed them into a system of wonderful complexity which regulated every duty of a Hebrew's life, and which hemmed him in from his waking in the morning until he went to sleep at night. And yet, according to Josephus, there never was a nation, as a nation, more completely given over to wickedness of every kind than this people, so abundantly supplied with moral precepts, and so instructed in the rigorous application of them to the least details of life.

What was needed was the power of example, to infuse into men a new spirit, a spirit which could dispense with all this cumbrous machinery and, laying hold of the great principles, proceed to apply them in the calm power of personal conviction and loving imitation. This Christ gave. While He does not avoid instruction—nay, while He is perpetually busied in giving it, it is the Son of Man who is made the centre of all. The foundation of the Sermon on the Mount, that without which it would have been as powerless to raise men as the many kindred utterances to which thought and love had led men before, was the command which takes shape on another occasion:

"Take my yoke upon you, and learn of me; for I am meek and lowly of heart; and ye shall find rest unto your souls. For My yoke is easy and My burden is light."

It is this peculiarity of our Lord's teaching which shapes, indeed which makes, our Christian year. Too deeply imbued with the spirit of Christ's teaching to forego an advantage so priceless—knowing that when Christianity becomes a mere system of doctrines the life is gone out of it—aware of the tendency of the human mind towards reducing moral and religious truths to mere formulæ—she brings back to our minds with unwearying patience the great outward *facts* in which truth has found its most eloquent expression. She is not content to leave her children, rich and poor, learned and unlearned, those who can think and those who have never been taught to think, indiscriminately, to the chances of remembering or forgetting the events of Christ's life. Their religious instructor may, if he be so forgetful of his ordination vow, preach only cold morality, or fanaticism, or dark, abstruse doctrines of predestination, or intoxicating dreams of mysticism. Not so the common Mother. To all her children, because all must have it or die, she sets forth in order the pure teaching of the Gospel. Nor is she content even with reciting to the ear in the daily lessons, the story of the Saviour's life, or the words of Him who spake as never man spake. To the imagination, that mightiest lever of the moral world, she addresses the silent utterances of her wisely ordered seasons. By festival and fast, by seasons of mourning and seasons of rejoicing, she drives home the lessons taught by the various events of the spotless life of her Master, by the descent of the Holy Ghost, and by the manifestation ever and anon of the three Persons of the blessed Trinity. By this perpetual reminder of the events of His earthly life she combats the tendency to lose sight of the historical Man, Christ Jesus. She puts it beyond the power of any teacher to deprive his flock of what is needful for their spiritual sustenance. In spite of himself he must preach Jesus Christ and Him crucified.

But there is another set of influences, which although of inferior importance, is full of value. Had Christ's life passed as unsuccessfully during after time, as to human eyes at least, it did during His actual ministry, it would be hard for any one to begin now the imitation of it. We need to be reminded of the breadth of meaning in those words of the creed which teach us that the Holy Catholic Church is the communion of Saints. We are not to be deprived of the comfort and encouragement that flow from the knowledge that, however fruitless for the time, were His words, His love and His example, His followers awoke when He was ascended into Heaven, to all that He had been to them, and found in that invisible fellowship which is ours as much as theirs, the courage to build up and consecrate with their blood, the Church that He had founded. Nor among those alone who enjoyed His earthly companionship, but among all Saints of all ages, yea among all Angels, have we a right to mingle in spiritual communion, for the rousing of our drooping souls and the quickening of our hopes. But if so, how is it to be taught? By leaving every man to his own devices here?—by trusting that the power of such influences will be sufficiently valued to dispense with reminders, when even our Master's example needs to be perpetually brought before us by fast and festival? Such a course would be strangely inconsistent. Therefore we have, applied to the object of keeping alive this class of influences, the same means which every Churchman finds by experience to be full of profit in preserving fresh the memory of the Saviour's life: therefore we have, scattered throughout the year, such festivals as that for whose celebration we are met to-day.

St. Matthew! you say, What profit is there for me in specially commemorating the life of St. Matthew? As the author of the first Gospel, as a godly and inspired man, certainly worthy of respect—certainly worthy to be made the subject of thankfulness to God. But as the traditional Evangelist of Ethiopia, Media, or Persia, the figure is too vague and shadowy to invest with much personal interest, Of St. Paul and St. John I know something. To their memories I am ready to devote a tribute of reverence! But St. Matthew does not stand to my mind as the symbol of any thing in particular; and I do not see the advantage of keeping a festival or going to church in his honor.

Read the Gospel for St. Matthew's day, I answer, and you will see abundant reason why he should stand to your mind as the symbol of something in particular. "And as Jesus passed forth . . He saw a man named Matthew sitting at the receipt of customs: and He saith unto him, 'Follow me.' And he arose and followed Him." What a picture is that! The despised and degraded tax-gatherer, excluded from the company of decent society by the odium gathering round his detested calling, and consorting with publicans and sinners, hears the kind voice that whispers to his mind of purity and a better life, and in simple devotion and gratitude abandons thenceforward his gainful calling to become the sharer of Christ's wandering, toilsome, thankless life. *That* a shadowy ghost, lack-

ing the distinctness necessary to call it up before the mind !
That a memory which the Church of God can afford to lose
from her roll of saintly heroes !   *That* an example with no
value for you in an age like this, when the wisest and the
purest find it hard to resist the covetous desires and inordinate love of riches which choke the word so often and
render it unfruitful !   Why, if there be one lesson more
than another which is needful for our day it is this—that
we must struggle against the love of ease and wealth, if we
would keep ourselves pure, and live the higher life to
which Christ calls us.   Everywhere the temptation
creeps in.   The poorest are infected by the poison of soul,
and sacrifice personal self-respect and decency to flaunt
their absurd finery in the House of God, while they pinch
themselves of necessaries, and run in debt to purchase
them.   It is this disposition to worship only money, and
what money buys, that brings about the envy and jealousy
of class against class, so accursed and unchristian when
they exist.   It is this inordinate love of riches that makes
men begin to toil for them as boys, before they have gotten any thing which can be called an education ; and so
robs their whole life of the refining and ennobling influence
of books.   It is this that is suffered to drain the body of
health, and the soul of its best powers, and so often ends
before middle life is reached, by using up brain and nerves,
and leaving the man a peevish, useless invalid, with no
higher aim than sensual enjoyment, and not health enough
to allow him that.   Need I follow the subject further into
society, and its harmful influence there in making the
young of both sexes marry for wealth and position only, in
sending them to live in hotels, instead of having homes of
their own when they do marry ;—into political life, and its

power there to make unworthy men or rulers, and to engross us so completely with our private money-getting that
we cannot spare time to oust the thieves, and put, and keep
honest men in office? To one who looks at the facts there
seems only too much melancholy truth in the Apostle's
words, "The love of money is the root of all evil."

If there be any truth then, in what I have said, I need
hardly urge, that to celebrate in its true spirit the festival
of St. Matthew, is a most timely protest against the perpetual festival of Mammon which we celebrate with such
devotion. This day which brings forcibly to our hearts
the truth that there are higher things in life than a good
income, which tells us that a man has been upon earth
who could deliberately abandon wealth and its pursuit
when a better thing was put before him, who was clear-
sighted enough to prize peace and love and gratitude to
Christ above money, and pure-hearted enough to abide by
such a decision—what a day ought it to be to all of us,
whether poor or rich who keep it!

And remember that there are more ways than one of
keeping it. Regarding the Holy Communion itself the
Church teaches us, in the rubric after the Office for the
Communion of the sick that "if a man by reason of
extremity of sickness, . . . or by any other just impediment, do not receive the Sacrament of Christ's Body
and Blood, the Minister shall instruct him that if he do
truly repent him of his sins, and steadfastly believe that
Jesus Christ hath suffered death upon the Cross for Him,
and shed His Blood for his redemption, earnestly remembering the benefits he hath thereby, and giving Him hearty
thanks therefore, he doth eat and drink the Body and
Blood of our Saviour Christ profitably and to his soul's
health, although he do not receive the Sacrament with his

mouth." This teaching, throwing so strong a light as it does upon the Church's *spiritual* view of the Holy Communion, is worthy of constant remembrance just now. But a similar view is applicable to the matter in hand. It would be foolish and unreasonable to demand or expect all to abandon the busiest part of the day, to give up what would be, in many cases, the whole of it, as a workman or employé must do, to attend public worship. I neither expect it, nor desire it of all. It is for every man to ask himself whether the impediment which keeps him from Church is a *just* one, though I am sure that if all came who were not *justly* and really hindered, the Church would be well attended. But if you cannot come here, that is no reason why you should not take time to read the service appropriate to the day, to offer up its beautiful collect, and above all, earnestly strive from morning till night to keep in your mind, and act upon, the lesson taught by it, and so terribly needed by us all. It will keep you from being wholly absorbed in business. If you lose, it will help you to bear loss, by its teaching of the higher value of self-control and submission. It will encourage you to struggle against the spirit that grovels in the love of lucre, and overcome it. It will raise you above the present, with its tumult and passion, and bring before you, from the distant past, in its serene and majestic completeness, the rounded life of a man who actually has trod the earth, who actually overcame your temptations, and who now rests from earthly trial among the saints in Paradise. You may be justly hindered from praying in a Church of human building, but if so, in the sanctuary of a chaste breast and quiet mind, you may keep as truly and as profitably, the good old festival of St. Matthew. Take home then the spirit of the day.

XI.

THE CENTURION AT CAPERNAUM.

HOW CAN I WORK?

"The centurion answered and said: Lord, I am not worthy that thou shouldest come under my roof; but speak the word only and my servant shall be healed."—ST. MATTH. viii. 8.

THE centurion at Capernaum is a remarkable figure among the characters brought before us in the Gospels. From the accounts given in the Gospel of St. Matthew, and in that of St. Luke, we piece together a conception of the man something like this. He was a Roman officer who had been long enough stationed in Palestine to have had his attention attracted by the religion of the Jews. Even in that out-of-the-way station on the shores of the sea of Tiberias, among a population too poor to build a synagogue for themselves, mainly composed of fishermen, and probably little calculated to make a Roman soldier lay aside that contempt with which the Jews were commonly regarded by their conquerors, he had had the spiritual insight and liberality of mind to see how vastly superior were the principles of their religion to any thing he had met with elsewhere. Contrasting their creed, and the evidence of a written revelation on which it was based, with the cruel, or superstitious, or revolting religions of pagandom, he had seen the imposing majesty of their belief in one God, the Creator and the Father of the world. Nor had he pursued the investigation of the subject merely as one of curious interest.   He had probably connected himself, as a proselyte of the gate, with the Jewish congregation in the village.   This appears likely from the report given by the elders of the Jews in St. Luke's version of the story: " He loveth our nation and hath built us our synagogue " (for the original implies that this was the only place of worship they had).

Now, for a Roman soldier to act in this way shows very remarkable qualities—qualities that prepare us for the commendation bestowed by our Saviour on his unexampled faith.   The Romans generally looked upon religions other than their own with contemptuous indifference.   In their view religion was important mainly as connected with the state, and with the duties men owed to the state.   Hence the endeavor on the part of the Roman rulers to keep up the outward observances of their religion after they had entirely ceased to believe in it themselves.   Hence the frantic efforts made by the best of their emperors to restore it when it had well-nigh died out, thinking that external observance of its forms would satisfy the gods, and impart new vigor to their rapidly decaying institutions. But here was a man who not only was ready to believe that other religions might have deep meaning for a soldier of the mighty empire, but actually had trained himself into a complete and unquestioning faith in the most despised of all religions, that of the hated Jews.

The circumstances of his life, too, must not be left out of the account.   Ordinarily, as we know, the profession of arms does not help to make men religious.   Even the constant risk of death to which soldiers are exposed, instead of increasing the activity of conscience, and keeping before the mind the interests of eternity on whose brink they are continually standing, has, in general, the effect of hardening the moral sense, and banishing serious thoughts. Such a life as that which lay before the centurion, is perhaps, even more unfavorable to religion than actual warfare. The absence of occupation generally inclines men in camp or garrison life to kill time by vicious amusements; and their associates are rarely such as to stimulate them to any higher occupations. The centurion, however, appears to have resisted and overcome such temptations as his profession exposed him to. He had thoughtfully studied the religion of the inhabitants, had actively employed himself for their improvement, and had given largely to provide them the opportunity of public worship which they were too poor to provide for themselves. Certainly, under the circumstances, a most noteworthy person. No wonder that when his request was made known to Christ He should have marvelled, and said that He had not found so great faith, no, not in Israel. For the centurion does not appear to have drunk in the prejudices of his new religion, but only its good, and to have been led by what he had learned of its promises much further than his teachers. Whether he fully believed, at this time, in Christ as the Messiah we cannot tell; but he seems, at all events, to have believed frankly and undoubtingly that Jesus was the messenger of God, and able to perform miracles such as only the highest prophets of Israel had ever wrought. The sense of Christ's dignity was high enough to make him feel that his house was unworthy of being honored by the Saviour's presence, and we are induced to suppose that as he certainly had heard of Christ's claims he must have fully accepted them as well-founded.

I have dwelt at such length upon this man, who after once appearing, is heard of no more in the Gospels, partly because I am persuaded that a great deal of the teaching power of the Bible lies in its giving us in actual narrative —in its vividly-drawn characters—specimens of almost all varieties of spiritual experience. And further, much of this is lost from the unthinking way in which the Bible is too commonly read. I should certainly be far from wishing any one to read the Sacred Volume with less of reverence than he now feels—or with less conviction that all Scripture is given by inspiration of God. But there is a *kind* of reverence for it which causes those who cherish it to lose a vast deal of its benefit. Such persons seem to think, from the startled air they have when the freshness and naturalness of the Bible are presented freshly and naturally, that to make any particular *use* of it except to arouse the thought of God's glory and the solemnity of eternity, is almost profane. But surely if Christ was not averse to joining in the innocent occupations of daily and social life—if He was to be found in familiar intercourse with men at weddings and dinner-tables, not lowering Himself by so acting, but teaching men that whatever is not immoral is capable of being used and improved by the healthy, God-fearing soul—if He encouraged the freest and most unconstrained use of His loving wisdom to meet all difficulties for all men—if this be so, as unquestionably it is, then why should any one be afraid to use the Bible in the same way? And we do not so use it, unless we learn to look at its narrative part more particularly, as a bright, fresh, animated story of living events, long past indeed, but still living in their value for us. We must consider the men and women who figure in that fascinating narrative as persons who actually lived and breathed as we do, who had their own personal history made up, like ours to-day, of joys and sorrows—of doubts and struggles. And we must try to understand those experiences of theirs just as we try to comprehend those of any one now living to whom we are attached. This, I am sure, is the only way to get out of that wonderful, picturesque story of our dear Saviour's life, anything like the impression of His personal character which they got who were His daily companions. Don't be afraid of your Bible. Don't think that the only time to read it is in Church, or at family prayers, or when you feel especially solemn and want to work yourself up to some unnatural condition of soul. Look at it as intended for your soul's use at all times, and as capable of bringing you closer to your Lord than any amount of that spiritual excitement which cannot see that while we live on earth we must live in another way than by shutting our eyes to all the brightness, and beauty, and freshness that God has provided for our delight and cultivation.

Then your spirituality will be really higher, because it will fit in more naturally and easily with the common duties of life. Your Christianity will be healthier because it will not shut itself off from what belongs to an earnest life here on earth. Christ, Himself will seem nearer and easier to get at, when thought of as associating familiarly with people whom we feel almost acquainted with, than He ever can be when viewed *only* as sitting at the right hand of God. If He has been the kind, and gentle, and loving companion of other persons no wiser and no stronger than yourself, you will find it much less hard to ask Him to be your companion too, and will find yourself naturally thinking of Him when you are weak, or discouraged, or in trouble.

But it was not merely to introduce some much-needed counsel on reading the Bible that I chose this text, nor that I might make you feel that this Roman centurion, now so long since gone to his reward, once actually lived, not only in a book, but in flesh and blood, with thoughts, and duties, and sicknesses and anxieties. He lived, like the rest of us, to do something and make something out of his life here. In what we have already seen of his doings and thinkings, we may find help for our own discharge of the duty laid upon us.

And the first lesson is this—that even under the most unfavorable circumstances, one may get help from the surroundings of his daily life toward serving and knowing God. It is a piece of spiritual wisdom which comes very late to many of us,—the conviction that we were put into our particular place by God's special design, and that, inasmuch as He had all positions possible to choose among, and did choose just this one, it must be the one where we may best serve Him, and do good to our own souls. The trials and temptations to which our position exposes us may be very numerous. We may find it very hard work to keep up our spirituality under the temptations to impatience or discontent by which we are beset. But let us remember that there is no position in life to which the same, or similar objections do not apply. And the longing to be rid of these difficulties is very generally a longing to be rid of all which troubles us simply *because* it troubles us, and not because we are yearning after a larger opportunity of promoting God's glory. That is, it arises from weariness, and not from the pure spirituality for which we mistake it.

Look at the position of this Roman centurion. Could

any situation seem less likely to result in his growing wiser and purer than that in which he was placed? He had next to nothing to do in that little, out-of-the-way village, and idleness, as we know, is extremely apt to produce a crop of vices. There was no public worship there to attract a lazy officer, lounging about the hamlet trying to kill the time. There was only a set of poor people, not over-wise, or over-well-instructed even in their religion; and their religion was, from a number of circumstances, one of the last likely to attract a Roman officer. Put any ordinary man under circumstances like these, and you would say that the likelihood would be that he would grow slothful and inattentive to all but the mechanical duties of providing for the hundred men immediately under his charge— that he would treat the people among whom he was stationed with contemptuous indifference, if not with harshness—that, in a word, he would be ruined, body and soul, by a life so full of temptations to harm, so bare of inducements to purity and activity. Certainly, for most men, such would be the probability. Such is generally admitted to be a sadly common result among our own army officers when long stationed in small frontier posts, even with a much more close and frequent intercourse, through mails, with civilized life than was possible in those days. But such unpromising surroundings did not produce the result that might reasonably have been looked for. Why not? For no reason that I can think of but because he would not *let* them corrupt him; because he *fought* against the bad influences that imperilled his character—making duties, and learning to take interest in the people around him —learning from them all that he could, and trying to benefit them in return. Was there but little for him to do? He made work for himself. Was it wearisome to have no companionship but that of soldiers, and poor, ignorant villagers? He set to work, and found that poor, ignorant villagers were men needing help, and that could understand, and be grateful for kindly interest in their welfare.

When you take into account that this man had not, to begin with, even so much knowledge of God as the Jewish religion in its then condition could convey to him, I think we may readily believe that no one here has so unpromising a situation in life—unpromising, I mean, for advancement in religious knowledge and grace. Yet see what he made out of his position; even surprising Christ Himself by the purity and depth of his belief; by the humbleness of his character; by his readiness to accept Him and what He promised.

Now I do not mean to underrate the actual difficulties of any man's lot. I know what a weary feeling is produced by the burden of uncongenial duty. Poverty is hard to bear; unkindness is hard. Selfishness and ill-temper, folly, and vice, and crime on the part of those with whom we are closely connected by blood or marriage—all these are among the most disheartening things which any one can have to endure. And trying as they are at the time, it is, if possible, worse yet to look forward to the future, and see there no prospect of relief for many a year to come, if ever in this life. What I do mean to say is this: these things did not happen by chance. Your lot, just such as it is, saving so far as you yourself may have made it worse, was carefully arranged by a God whose love and wisdom you dare not say you doubt. If anything in heaven or earth be true, then it is true that this lot was allowed, in all its features, both those for which you are, and those for which you are not responsible, in order that you might be purer and holier. If you are not growing purer and holier it must be your own fault. In that earthly lot which you grumble over, there lies all that is needed to make you better. Is it not worth while to give up, once for all, your whinings and lamentations and take God at His word? Poverty and sickness, sorrow and vexation are not likely to become any easier excepting in one way—that of submitting to them and trying to make the best of them as being God's carefully chosen discipline for your improvement. We all know the cheerful serenity which others have won by this line of conduct. We have all seen people who were not only bright and contented, but positively happy, under circumstances more hard to bear than our own. So that this lesson which I am expounding from the Centurion's story cannot be considered one of those self-satisfied pieces of useless good advice with which the pulpit is often credited by people who imagine that a clergyman is ignorant of the real trials and temptations of life. It forms the burden of much of the Bible's teaching: it is in thorough agreement with the whole tenor of our Saviour's history on earth : it is the only way in which any man can prevent God's ordinary plan of administering the affairs of this world from seeming a cruel and meaningless mockery. Are these reasons enough for my thinking there must be a deal of truth in it, and for my imploring you to see whether it will not suit your case?

But the centurion's words chosen as our text contain an example of the only hopeful way in which the lesson I am trying to enforce can be used. Apart from Christ, one kind of discipline is as little likely to give us *God's* peace as another. There are instances in the world's history of men who just by stern determination, and without any belief in a God or a Providence have crushed down the cry of weariness that rises naturally to the lips of one oppressed with care and hopeless of a brighter future. But such instances are so very rare that I should think it useless to urge any ordinary person to follow their example. And even if it were possible for us all to repress our misery, so far as any outward exhibition of it is concerned, the inner condition in which we should still remain would be but a very dreary and ghastly one. It is the peace of *God*, which passeth understanding that we all need : and that never has been—never can be—attained in such ways as this. For our hearts feel, and were meant to feel. Anything that has for its deliberate purpose to freeze them up and hinder their true working, is only another name for suicide—suicide of the best part of our nature. And the number of those who have nerve enough to kill their hearts is, God be thanked, as small as the number of men who can coolly take poison or blow out their brains, when not driven wild by agony or fear. It is a hopeless thing for all but one or two in a million ; and it is as useless in fact as it is hopeless, to tell them to submit and make the best of their lot, without telling them how this is to be done—how it has been done.

When the centurion asked Christ to help him, he did not make the application in vague hope that now, after all other means, had failed to cure his servant, it might be worth while to try Christ's power, as something which, if it did no good, could at all events do no harm. If he had come in such a spirit as that, it is not likely that he would have obtained what he wanted. Quite different was his course. He was so deeply persuaded of the Saviour's dignity that he would not even ask Him to enter his house: "Lord, I am not worthy that thou shouldst enter under my roof; but speak the word only and my servant shall be healed." He had no doubt at all on the subject. And so the Lord could say unto him: "As thou hast believed so be it done unto thee." His reward was in exact proportion to his faith: as this was boundless so was that. "And his servant was healed in the self-same hour."

The treatment of those who applied to Christ for help was always like this. His common way of answering such applications was: "Thy faith hath saved thee: go in peace." Now the troubles of which I have been speaking as so sorely demanding self-discipline are, even more than the bodily ills in relieving which Christ spent so much of His time, of just the kind that need faith in Him for their relief. They cannot be cured in an instant. The bitterness and the weariness which come of discontent, the sourness that springs from impatient bearing of the faults of others, the selfishness which wants all of a sudden to overleap discipline, and win at once the peace God promises— all these have grown in many a case into very deeply rooted diseases, and have established themselves in our natures by years of indulgence. It may take a long period of Lenten discipline for them to be thoroughly gotten rid of. But they can be rooted out. The whole purpose of Christ's mission on earth is misunderstood—the whole nature of the Spirit's agency upon human character is overlooked—by one who does not believe that all things are possible with God —yes even such wonders as this of which I am speaking. The Holy Spirit puts into our minds good desires, and works with us when we entertain them. From first to last we are His workmanship, created in Christ Jesus unto good works, which God hath before ordained that we should walk in them. If you are shamed by the spectacle of what this true-hearted centurion did under circumstances so very unfavorable—if you have at this moment a feeling that it is your duty to conquer the impatience and discontent that make your life so dark and comfortless— why, that is the movement of God's Spirit in your heart, and it is for you not to let it die away. It is thus, commonly, that He works. He gives a little light, and then, if we use it, He gives us more. He aids us in the most quiet way possible—so quietly that often men do not think of Him as being with them at all—to make the first attempt. Then, after the resolution is made, there comes a trial to test it. If the impulse to overcome the temptation be acted upon, more strength is given for the next occasion of difficulty. But if not—if you give up because you seem to have nothing but yourself to rely upon,—then you fall back into the same hopeless, heartless state you were in before. God does not mean that you should forget your share in the great work of conquering yourself; and so He *generally* leaves you to believe in His help, not actually to see it—and He leaves a great deal to your belief. It is a long time before you can *see* Him working with you. But it is always given at last to one who can both work and quietly wait for it. And then you find, almost to your surprise, how much has been accomplished while you have been steadily plodding along. The Spirit has been quietly working in you, revealing more of Christ, disclosing more of His love, and awakening a responsive feeling in your heart; and so, without any violent convulsion or excitement, you have become strong instead of weak, believing instead of faithless. The great miracle has been wrought while you have been looking for it.

Such, dear friends, is the general course of God's Spirit and the influence of Christ. If you have some such task in your own life, I cannot promise you the victory from anything but patient work. First believe that God meant you to be a true Christian, and that the means for becoming one lie all around you; and there can be no doubt that his purpose will finally become a reality. The word *has* been spoken: it rests with you whether you shall be healed.

XII.

STRENGTH IN THE LORD.

" My brethren, be strong in the Lord and in the power of His might."
—EPH. vi. 10.

WEAKNESS, real or fancied, is the great bane, the great
hindrance of our lives. It acts in many ways. The
wrongs that we would fain see righted, in the world, in
the Church,—wrongs, that we too should combat if we felt
ourselves stronger, live on their hateful lives and blast
generation after generation. Inner defects whose daily-
recurring manifestation begets a fatal torpor and nerveless
despair, find their strongest tenure of existence in the
notion that after so many fruitless attempts we should be
foolish again to pit our feebleness against their might.
The noble aspiration after growth in knowledge and holiness
is in some moods almost smothered because we permit ourselves so little to estimate the spiritual forces at our command. In this way, I verily believe, one may be actually
harmed by thinking too much about the glories laid up for
us in heaven. Looking out from the field of daily life with
its pitiful successes and crushing reverses to that state to
which we hope to come, one may be enervated rather than
stimulated—one may positively turn what is meant to encourage into an excuse for inactivity, under the false impression that what we are sure after all to gain need
hardly be striven for now with much intensity. To moods
like these St. Paul's words come with strange, arousing

142

power. You are strong, he says, if you would only believe it. Defeat is out of the question if only you will learn to feel that victory is rightfully yours. This state of morbid depression is only a kind of hypochondria of which you will be rid as soon as you resolve upon it. Here lies the strength you want. Take it and use it. Be strong in the Lord and in the power of His might.

The strength that comes from another character is what the world offers us as the nearest approach to the truth St. Paul would here enforce regarding our soul's lives. No one can be completely ignorant of it in his own experience. It is said that the boldest men confess to fear when they first get under fire; and that it is only by the sense of comradeship, and above all by the example of their leaders that they come to the condition in which regard for their personal safety gives way to resolute intrepidity. So it certainly is in many of the commoner experiences of life. To see another undertaking and performing tasks for which we have felt ourselves unfit,—this partly shames, but more largely cheers us to do them too. I believe that many Christians who would be seriously embarrassed in their religious lives by the difficulties of believing, are helped to exercise a larger and more salutary faith from seeing that others, whom they know to be not only wise but honest, share the same difficulties, and yet find a practical solution for them in unreserved trust in God's truth. Here indeed, lies, for the large number, one of the most important uses of the Church, and particularly of those in it who, known to be honest and capable, grapple fearlessly with great problems, and show that with all their reality they are not fatal to the deepest conviction. Troubled over this doctrine, or that dispensation, you look backward or around you, and see how great intellects and pure souls have borne these burdens, and you strengthen yourself with their strength, recognizing indeed, your own feebleness, but drawing from the spectacle of their demeanor the power to rise above difficulty, and from a loftier standing-point to behold the truth, which before, you despaired of gaining.

These are types only, and very imperfect hints, of the strength which St. Paul tells us we may have in the might of God. They only suggest to us one or two of the ways in which this latter may operate upon ourselves. Let us examine some of them.

One strengthens himself in God's strength in the first place negatively, by getting rid of so much of the discouragement arising from his past as comes from failure. That failure, we are all aware, comes from ourselves, not from Him. The temptation you yielded to yesterday you know would not have overcome you had you not either trusted overmuch in your own power to resist it, or failed at the moment of its onset to fall back on God. I think we may even detect, as we look into the motions of our minds on some occasions, an almost deliberate and purposed shutting out of the warning thought that His eye is upon us, and His presence with us, to give needful strength if only we will have it. The doubts or even the convictions we have reached about the wrongfulness of a deed may be deliberately brushed aside, and all the lessons of past experience voluntarily overlooked, to give up ourselves anew to what we are sure is wrong. This is an extreme case; but something of this kind I think we must all own to in every instance of wrong-doing. We have not tried to strengthen ourselves in the power of Our

Father's might. Now this is discouraging enough from one point of view. What we have so often done we may do again. But it is cheering too if thus, through the conviction that our failure is not unavoidable, we reach the resolution to avail ourselves hereafter of what we have hitherto neglected. If we can lay firm hold upon the readiness and the sufficiency of God's might for all our needs, we may make a fresh beginning, and start upon a path so much the more hopeful as we are not weighed down by the discouragement of past defeats. In the possibility of this lies the grand, the imperishable cheerfulness of the Christian life. No matter what may have been our want of success, just in so far as we have brought it upon us by neglect of the right means, in that proportion may the dearly-bought knowledge of what are the right means nerve us to fresh and more courageous beginnings. And as every failure is directly traceable to this mistake, there is hardly an end to the new starts we may make, should we still fail from time to time. I know the danger that lies in this way of speaking. I know the possibility for every one of us of so wresting this truth as to yield with less resistance, knowing that we may have another chance; and that this danger will not be wholly done away by the other certainty, that there is a state to be reached even in this life, where there remaineth no more place for repentance though we seek it carefully with tears. But capable though it be of such a wresting, it is a glorious and necessary truth; one without which the cheerfulness characteristic of all noblest lives would be impossible— without which all hope must be cut off from every purest soul who through the weakness of our mortal nature was still not wholly purged from sin. This then, is the first

7

of the ways in which we are to strengthen ourselves in the might of God. We are to remember that His power, not our own as before, is the main-stay, the sole support, of our endeavors. Who does not feel how utterly different a face this puts upon the whole warfare! Who that lays hold upon it does not feel himself able to step forward with new confidence in the performance of duty, knowing now what lay at the root of old defeat, and conscious of the strength of God's right arm in every blow he deals at the enemies of his soul!

Then again, such a strengthening is curiously wrought when the truth comes home to us that He is thus made more unmistakably our champion—thus appears more clearly on our side. Let me try to make this plain; for forgetfulness of it explains much that is strange in the non-realization of the promises vouchsafed us. Even when one has almost wholly outgrown the bitter feeling that *calamity* is proof of God's being against us—even when one has reached the power to submit to great trials, there still remains a temper very closely akin to it in our way of looking at the Christian life at large—its disciplinary character and ceaseless struggle, the intermittent peace, the slow advance, which indeed, do not necessarily belong to it so far as God's willingness goes, but which as a matter of fact, are its universal features in a greater or less degree. I do not mean at all that noble discontent with ourselves which, here at least, is inseparable from improvement, and which never lets us rest in our strivings after something better. Nor again, are we to blame that longing for rest in the bosom of God which must flow from our natural weariness as well as from the purest love for Him. None of these is blame-worthy or misleading. But the question is: "How do you habitually feel toward God in view of all these things?" Is it your usual way to feel that the furthering of your spiritual life is an end desired *in common* between yourself and Him, sought by a mutual understanding, so to speak, as the sick man's recovery is by himself and his physician, each thoroughly understanding the other and working patiently together upon a plan agreed upon in full comprehension of the case and of the only way to treat it? If this were common, I think we should see more traces of it. I see the opportunity of rendering more easy and permanent, its attainment by each soul, in that strengthening in the might of God of which St. Paul speaks. It makes all the difference in the world whether you simply submit to discipline, however resignedly, or take that active share and interest in God's treatment which I have tried to picture by the relation between the willing and understanding patient and his physician. Learn this lesson thoroughly—come to view the common aspect of your spiritual life in the same way as that in which the sick man regards the minute prescriptions and troublesome round of treatment at any sanitary establishment, and you will have toward God, the arranger of it, something of that unreserved trust, that affectionate reliance—you will win from Him some of the strength which comes to a sufferer when he thinks of the wise healer who is thus building up a disordered and weakened system. Convinced, as we may be in general, of the need of some such arrangement as we actually find for cleansing our souls, perhaps there are none who do not lose much by the unconscious adoption of the view that this particular trial might have been dispensed with, or that particular blessing granted, if God had really been on our side, thoroughly and heartily—if our interests were as tenderly cared for as He has said. We do not put such feelings into words; but there they lie festering at the roots of our common thought about God, hindering us from strengthening ourselves as we might. But try to root out this unworthy, weakening thought; learn by prayer and effort to get out of the range of this blind, selfish feeling; strive to make habitual the instinct that you are indeed working along with God, and He with you; and there will come a strength which is based upon His might, makes use of it, triumphs by means of it, wins sustenance from the environment of trial and sorrow in which every human life has its being. This is what Luther so finely says in the last verse of his famous hymn, although it is utterly absent in its terse vigor from both the common translations, so that I must render it for you:

> " He's with us on the field of strife,
>   With all His gifts and graces."

I am conscious that this matter of which I am speaking is one so subtle that it is hard to make it quite clear; but it is a very real matter; the lack of this feeling of Gods being always and wholly on our side, with unerring wisdom and yearning love, is common and harmful to the last degree. And I have no need to show you that if we do win such an habitual way of feeling towards Him, we shall strengthen ourselves in His might in a manner that will put a very different aspect on our lives. The theory, if I may so speak, of the Christian life as put before us in the Bible is, that the regenerated soul, with its higher instincts awakened, and eternal glory laid hold of as its rightful inheritance, works along with God, feels its intimate union with Him, trusting with a diviner instinct even where it cannot plainly see, unfaltering in the belief that sin is on the one side, and on the other God and His new-created children. Only on some such conviction can we live successfully. The ups and downs, the flagging energy, the fading visions of spiritual attainment, that mark most experiences, are traceable always, I think, to practically admitting discord to establish itself between us and the Author of all strength, looking suspiciously at Him, losing, in a word, the feeling I am speaking of, that He is always and unconditionally on our side. "My lot is hard," you say. "Life is gloomy and filled to overflowing by weary tasks that never come to an end, and never will until the great task we call life is over. Such weakness as mine can never avail to do more than to keep up the pretence of resistance. I will not actually throw down my arms and surrender; still less can I desert to the enemy by openly renouncing God's service; but I know that I shall go on yielding to wrong about as often as I have been doing; and your fine platitudes on the growth of Christian character have lost all their meaning, if meaning they ever had. God would help me, I suppose, if only I were so much better than I am as to be able to use His help; but as matters stand I do not see any signs of His caring for me, and it is a very shadowy faith that I have in the doctrine that ' all things work together for good.'" One often finds something like this in one's self or in others, and it shows well the consequences that come about when the faith is lost that God is with us. And, hopeless as such a condition seems to be—impossible as it seems to arouse one who has lost, or thinks he has lost, the power even to accept God's help, there is one remedy which often succeeds when hope is almost gone. God is love, yet He does not disdain to wake men by fear. So again, the distinctive feature of the Gospel is its elevating human character, and redeeming it from the hopelessness of self-loathing by giving it in the incarnate Christ a chance to respect itself; yet it does not shut out the sense of *shame.* Now, what lies at the bottom of all this moaning and whining about our souls—this pretence of having gone from Dan to Beersheba and found that all was barren? It comes from selfishness—from keeping our eyes perpetually turned in upon ourselves and our discomforts till we are like that most contemptible of all beings, a fancied invalid, upturning everything to gratify a foolish whim, and then complaining because it does not satisfy. Of what we are looking after, the spiritual life *is* barren, particularly when we so look. God's promises have no application to him who is mainly anxious, not to serve God, but to be comfortable. If such an one *could* use the power of the Lord's might to do more successfully that which he complains of having failed in, the result would be hardly commensurate with the means. It would be to foster just the selfishness which must be disappointed, in order that there may be aroused, before it is too late, that noble shame under whose influence the falser self slips from us like a robe, and we stand before God abashed yet strong, with hitherto unknown strength, in the consciousness that there is something better to live for. In a mood like this one learns many lessons that before were empty sounds; and none more thoroughly than this, that if God seems not to be on our side it is because we have left Him, and turned from the patient pursuit of holiness to the enervating search after self-pleasing. He will be with you soon· enough, and visibly enough, when you retrace your steps.

But St. Paul bids us be strong *in the Lord*, as well as in the power of His might. The ways in which, as I have been trying to point out, one may do the latter, are of the kind that come from setting right our views and feelings as to the manner in which life is to be led and duty done —remembering truths half-forgotten, and recognizing as on our side the Lord whom we had hidden from us by our selfishness. Deeply internal as such processes in one sense are, they are almost of an external and mechanical nature as compared with what the apostle means when he bids us be strong first of all in the Lord. The most unimpeded vision of all the truths I have been reminding you of—the fullest grasp of them as sublime and unquestionable facts, would avail nothing to one to whom they came with no union with God such as is meant by the deep phrase being in, or being strong in the Lord. So too, it would be almost useless to try to describe it to those who have had such knowledge and only suffered it to lose its immense importance. It is not a description of it then, that I shall try to make, but only a reminder of things we all know, when I speak in conclusion a few words about this matter, put so prominently by St. Paul in his farewell exhortation to the Ephesians. You have never, unless perhaps momentarily, confounded things so different as being in the Lord and being merely a member of the Church outwardly—professing Christ, and knowing Christ—discharging duty, and making yourself a living sacrifice to Him who redeemed you.

Both are needful, but the higher absorbs and necessarily implies the lower. Whether it came suddenly, or spread itself over a series of ripening years, the consciousness of a strange oneness with God in Christ through the Spirit makes the crowning glory, the very substance, of the life led by every redeemed soul. In some way you cannot account for, can hardly trace, there grew up a feeling of mysterious connection with Him, which it is the business of all the details of life to make more intense and constant. The Bible speaks of rewards and punishments because human language is powerless to express the thoughts of Christ when He turns from earthly things to speak of heavenly. A punishment no doubt it is when this divine, consoling presence of God in the heart loses its clearness, but when you are yourself you do not think of it as being a punishment, any more than the dying man thinks of death as a punishment for having broken the laws of health, and worn out his system before its time. You feel it as the dying out of the soul's vitality. With this you can do all things, and when it is at its full those words are no exaggeration. Without it one has the sensation of losing health, losing strength, losing life. Then it is, and only then, that the false moods overcome one of which I spoke before—then, that past failure gives the gloomy foreboding of continued and inevitable disaster—then, that God seems, as with Pharaoh's army, to take the other side—to take off our chariot-wheels, so that we drive them heavily. Here is a mysterious fact accomplished in our life: God has once embraced, adopted, regenerated us, He has given us this great blessing of known, felt union with Himself; and all our experiences, of bitter reproach and discouragement, as well as of grave, serene, solemn joy, unite to teach us that here lies the secret of our lives. Men may call it mysticism, self-deception—all the names by which ignorance derides the experiences and convictions that it is too low to conceive of; but one thing we know, that whereas

we had been blind once, we saw, and that whether diminished or augmented, that illumination is "yet the
fountain light of all our day, is yet the master light of all
our seeing." Increased too, and lessened, we have learned
that it may be. The laws by which it grows or wanes are
too clearly impressed upon our minds to need learning
them again. Neglect of communion with God, self-seeking,
whether of the kind just spoken of, or undue immersion in
the cares and business and pleasures of this life,—these we
have seen spreading gloom over our heavens and turning
to brass the earth beneath our feet. What need then—
what urgent need, that we should be awakened by the
trumpet voice of Paul to be strong in the Lord! At our
imminent peril we forget the essentially miraculous and
supernatural character of the life these souls of ours must
lead. Subject as it is to the ordinary laws which give the
harvest to him who sows, there is in the proportion and
the nature of this harvest something transcending all human imagination but that of him who knows it. Seeing
then that ye know these things, happy are ye if ye do them.
Happy in feeling incapacity melt away and courage take its
place—happy in regaining what the slow years have stolen
of spiritual health and serenity—happy above all, not in
your own restored peace alone, but in the knowledge that
even the heart of God throbs with a joy that He has put
into His creatures the power to bestow upon Him—the joy
of seeing another of the souls for whom Christ died, re-
turning more and more lovingly to His fatherly embrace.
"Therefore my brethren, be strong in the Lord and in the
power of His might."

7*   .

XIII.

CHRIST FOUND IN THE PATH OF DAILY DUTY.

"Simon Peter saith unto them, I go a fishing. They say unto him, We also go with thee. They went forth, and entered into a ship immediately; and that night they caught nothing."—St. John xxi. 3.

THE lives of few of us pass without being varied by great crises in which the soul is lifted out of the monotonous daily routine, and transported into a new and untried sphere. And no man who has gone through such an experience but has felt, when the crisis was past, a dull, aching sense of emptiness. In a state like this his eyes open wearily, morning by morning, on the old life, whose hours are to be passed in one unvarying course, made more intolerable by the memory of what has been, and now is no more. It seems, at such times, that we have been awakened to a sense of the vastness of life, only to be plunged again into a dull round of trivialities, which must crush out of us all the high capabilities of which we have but newly become conscious: the glimpse into the world of greatness renders the petty details of ordinary existence unendurable.

Such crises are of various kinds, and the reaction is different according to the character of that from which it arises.

After long loveless years, in which the dim cloud of indifference seemed to have settled over our life, we may have suddenly awaked to the sweet consciousness of human

154

sympathy and affection; and after basking for awhile in its precious glow, we may have seen the sun from which it came sinking slowly before our eyes behind the dark hills of death. About such an experience as this there is a blank hopelessness which no one can put into words—a despairing apathy to all human interests that reaches down to those deeps in the soul which no plummet of speech can fathom. And when the life that is in us begins to revive, and we look out on the world again, how very different it all appears from what it did under that golden radiance! How tastless are the occupations in which we once engaged, if with no keen enjoyment, at least without the breathless languor that fills us now!

Or again, it may be the descent from the heights of glory to which our first communion with Christ has lifted us, that works this effect upon our souls. We have been blessed with an almost superhuman rapture. As we walked along the pathway of life, we were lifted as it were to the seventh heaven and became lost in bliss; but when He whom we love abandons us for a moment, in order to try our faith, and produce in us that spiritual strength that grows by trust in an unseen Lord, then we stand like the Apostles on the mount of Olives gazing blankly into Heaven after their Master as their eyes lost Him in the clouds. The first feeling here is like that in the former case—a longing to lie down and die. We cannot bend our energies to the execution of our daily duties—we cannot go back as the disciples did, to our commonplace home, and in the hard, unfeeling crowd prepare ourselves for His second coming.

Now it was after an experience uniting both these peculiarities that St. Peter gave utterance to the words of the text. Any one who has carefully studied the latter parts of the Gospels which recount the events that took place after the Resurrection, has marked the feelings which filled the hearts of those seemingly deserted men. By ourselves indeed, accustomed as are our eyes to that unearthly radiance in which are bathed all the occurrences of those forty days, and knowing, as we do, how all was of a piece with what had gone before, the risen Jesus is recognized as the same who had led and loved His own sheep during the years of His earthly life. But to the eleven He was as dead. They could not believe that He was again alive after having yielded up His breath on the ignominious cross. Again and again we see this difficulty making its appearance. They thought that it was His ghost and not Himself. Even on the present occasion, we see clearly enough the awe that held them back from asking Him, " Who art thou ?" The testimony of their senses was that here was their Lord. The testimony of their minds was that it could not be. And it was plainly to end this conflict that our Saviour once and again exhibited to them the most decisive proofs that it was His veritable self. To the affrighted disciples : "Behold My hands and My feet, that it is I, Myself: handle Me and see, for a *spirit* hath not flesh and bones as ye see Me have." To the doubting Thomas : "Reach hither thy finger and behold My hands, and reach hither thy hand and thrust it into My side."

The feelings then, of Peter, if like those of his fellows, which we have no reason to doubt, were those of one who mourns for a dead friend; while on the other hand he doubtless felt profoundly the loss of that spiritual guide whom, with all the earnestness of his great, turbulent heart, he had sincerely adored. It is only when all this stands clearly before us that we can apprehend the emotions which filled him, the mingled regrets and loathing with which he was resolutely combating, when he determined to set himself at work once more. To all outward appearance he began life again just where he had left off. Who can tell the sinking of heart with which he sat down to mend those same nets which he was preparing to cast into the sea when the strange, lovely youth after whom his heart now yearned, passed by and bade him leave all and follow Him! No doubt to his neighbors this seemed but the natural result of a course of procedure so at variance with the dictates of worldly prudence. Very likely too, that rough untutored soul was hardly conscious of all that intercourse with Christ had given him—perhaps mourned over the hopes of earthly grandeur which had been so sadly dashed. But a hero he was, and a hero he proved himself, by that one act of determining not to waste his life in idle regrets. He had drunk too deeply at the fountain of the Saviour's wisdom not to have wrought into the very texture of his soul the truth that self-sacrifice—the surrender of darling plans or hopes, may become the foremost duty. "Take up thy cross and follow Me," was ringing in his ears; and so he went back, sadly we know, but with a stern determination, to his old life-work, feeling that after all, perhaps, the promise that he should become a fisher of men would never be fulfilled, but firm in his resolution to do his duty, come what might.

Heroism like St. Peter's, my friends, is what we want, every one of us. Heroism that can grapple with the mean, and the paltry, and the trivial,—that can do its duty under all circumstances, without murmuring over the hardness of its lot, or wishing that its fate had been to labor among other scenes, less dreary and less monotonous. Heroism that, once seeing where it has to work, sits resolutely down and mends the torn nets, preparatory to going out in the murky night, and toiling through the long watches, just because God has said, " There lies thy duty; do it."

Probably not one person here but has moments when feelings like those of Peter arise—moments when he longs, and struggles to free himself from the fetters which bind him to one corner in the great workhouse of the world. Let us then look for light to dispel these phantoms; let us try to see what are the reasons why the All-wise has allotted to us just our particular spot to toil in, and no other; let us endeavor to trace out some of the causes why so large a part of our lives must be filled up with these little things that so test our patience.

When we put Christianity side by side with the moral systems which preceded it, we are struck with one grand peculiarity. The most important graces of the soul are those which ought to be exercised in every-day life—all virtues indeed, find here their appropriate sphere. Every day you are called upon to practice that charity which thinketh no evil. Every hour a demand is made upon the faith which brings into close contact with the material world around you, the invisible Father and Ruler of all. Your dearest friend, your darling child, claim from you that patience and forbearance without which every man's hand would be against his neighbor.

On the contrary, the occasion for great deeds that blazon a reputation in the book of fame, come very rarely. If every man were a Washington, very few would have an opportunity to act the sublime part that has placed our great patriot's name high above those who might have emulated him, had their surroundings been somewhat other than they were.

Now, it is in the recognition of this fact that the peculiarity lies of which I have spoken. Other systems trained men, or tried to train them, for great crises that never came. For the little duties that fill each day to overflowing they left them to fit themselves.

We look back on the majestic panorama of ancient history, and are stirred to the very soul by the grand heroism which animated it, but we forget how different Roman life would appear if we could catch a glimpse of the sternness, and cruelty, and despotism which lie concealed beneath the surface of noble daring and self-devotion. Christianity, on the other hand, seeing how these same virtues can seldom be practised on so lofty a scale, sets itself to work to apply them where they are most wanted, in common, every-day life. It tells you that it is easy enough to summon up the energies to a great work when thousands are ready to applaud you if you succeed, or to hiss you if you fail; but that the real test of a true soul is to do these things in your own family, or in the society in which you live; to do them quietly, unobtrusively, without looking around to see if men's eyes are upon you. When you are a world's spectacle, a dozen lower motives may creep in and urge you on. When your left hand knoweth not what your right hand doeth, the eye of One whose sole approbation outweighs the plaudits or the jeers of a universe is upon you, and then your reward is something for which an immortal soul may well strain every nerve.

This then, dear friends, is one reason why you are called upon to labor in an obscure corner among petty duties; because they are obscure and petty, and they show that the work is done for " the great Task-master's eye," and not for human praise. It is recorded that in the early days of art workmen were wont to bestow the most sedulous care on those hidden parts of a temple on which no human eye was to rest, "for the gods see everywhere." Your life is a temple; and while lofty column and delicate capital should present an aspect that must win the admiration of mankind, remember that it is in the slow, careful elaboration of the secret shrine where none can penetrate, that your sincere devotion to God is to be most plainly exhibited. If you were to set yourself to work, in that boastful spirit which tempts you to desert your dark, humble sphere, at some such achievement as you are burning to undertake, very likely your strength would fail just when it was most wanted. Peter was loud in his promises of what he would do, but contrast his bearing when he said, " Though I should die with Thee yet will I not deny Thee," with the self-loathing with which, when the foul denial had been uttered, he went out and wept bitterly.

No. The duty which is laid upon you, *that* you can perform. But do not long for some higher sphere in which you may display your fidelity, unless you desire to have that divine, sorrowful face turned upon you with its speechless depth of rebuke. Then you will long, more earnestly than you now wish to be called up higher, that you were sitting by Peter, mending those nets that now so weary you, and bending yourself with passionate, sorrowful activity to the performance of what alone you *can* do.

Again, suppose that the future Apostle, instead of manfully doing what his hand found to do, had listlessly sat down to dream of what had taken place during his life with Christ. Suppose he had gloomily meditated on the words that had so often fallen from the Saviour's lips—the unfulfilled promises of glory and a kingdom which had seemed so strangely to contrast with the humility and poverty in which his Lord's life had been spent, and to give some color to the royal expectations which were connected with the Messiah. Can we not see how all this would have drained him of the energy which he now so much needed? Can we not see that it would have sapped the foundations of his faith, and made him a useless dreamer, unfitted for his duties by the very experience that was intended to foster in him the growth of all true manliness? Contact with the living truth would thus have made him false, hollow, as unfit for any good end as the salt of the Master's parable, useless for the land or for the dung-hill, to be cast out of men.

A feature of the reaction already spoken of, and one of its most pernicious features, is the tendency often connected with it, to throw aside all exertion, and let our days slip by in reveries on the past and its possibilities. A host of excuses present themselves readily enough, and favored by our disinclination to rise from our indolence, they hang like a leaden weight on the arm which should be at honest work. True it is that we are enfeebled by the shock to our inner system, true that very little strength is left. But the question is not, " Will you wait till you are stronger, or over-tax your exhausted powers?"; but, "Will you do what you can, or lose the strength you have by doing nothing?" Nowhere is it of more vital importance so far to forget the things which are behind that you may reach forward to those that are before. Do not, indeed, forget, if you have learned it, that there is such a thing as pure, unselfish love on earth. Do not forget, if you have once enjoyed it, what it is to have Christ walking by your side, and filling your soul with holy love and hope. But, on the other hand, do not suffer a vision which was accorded you that you might be more loving and more holy, to fill you with misanthropy, or faithlessness. Let the love that you have tasted strengthen you to show to others that love, whose discovery changed your own life from one of selfishness to one of all-embracing charity. Instead of hiding in a napkin that talent committed to your care, the undying tenderness of Christ,—work out that lesson in each little act of every day. If for awhile the Saviour is lost to your sight, show that you know Him to be very near to you by faith, teach every one around you to believe in the possibility of God's love by displaying that which bears so close a resemblance to it, the love of a man. For there are many in this wide world of ours, who never know what it is to have a gleam of human sympathy shining in on their darkness. All around you there are souls that would welcome a face of wise, kindly, human interest, as you would welcome that of an angel. Hardened by the terrible struggle for daily bread, they are not so hardened that they cannot understand that it is something sent from heaven to them, when one comes and takes their hand, and utters a few words of gentle, human cheer, and does one little deed to show that those words are not lies, like all the rest they hear. O, it is base to let your powers rust uselessly, embittering your own life, when they might be so nobly employed in making plain to some dwarfed, stunted soul, that there is something to strive for besides food for the body. Waiting, forsooth, for some great task which shall summon up all your energies, and be worthy of them! Well, here is a task which is not a little one surely, nor an ignoble one, since for this very end the Son of God lived and died. Go out and see whether this is not the work you are made for. At all events, better this than nothing. Better this than idly waiting for an opportunity which may never come, while all the time, nearer, nearer, nearer, speeds that great day when you shall give an account of the deeds done in the body.

And after all, where do we get the right to call these deeds little and paltry and insignificant? What gives its character and complexion to an act? We assume, in thus speaking that it is the way in which men look at it, and admire it,—that it is the number of eyes bent upon him who performs it, the number of voices that unite in singing his praises. But will such a standard do? How many eyes looked on the poor widow who cast her mites into the treasury of God? One. But that one was worth all. That one was looking not at the amount of the gift, but at the wealth of self denial and trust in God, of which the outward deed was the symbol and exponent. How many think you would have heard of the tender love of that nameless woman, who in her tender solicitude of Christ, brought the box of ointment to anoint Him beforehand to the burial—how many would have heard of her had not the quick eye of the Lord seen what was in her heart, and recorded it in words that shall never lose their lustre while the world shall stand? Those were great deeds, we think, and one whose moral sight is undimmed will not hesitate to rank them with the loftiest achivements of the world's loftiest heroes. But it is not that we praise them. That gives them no additional glory. They were great when they were performed ; great when they were conceived, and the heart where they arose swelled with powers as great as any which are now rusting idly for want of some noble task.

It was that inner character that led the Saviour to set on them His royal signet. And on *every* such act—on every quiet deed of love or self-denial—on every word of kindliness or cheer—on each and all of these rests just the same halo of the Master's approval. Would you win His favor—would you have the consciousness that His eye rests on you with the same glance as that which cheered the bearer of the alabaster box? Go thou and do likewise. Men may not know of it. Better so. You will be saved from the temptation of doing it to gain their applause.

But the universe of God is a whispering-gallery through which no lowest word from the lips of pitying love, but resounds in thunder-tones through heaven's hosts, far, far up to the great white throne. The loud plaudits of men you can dispense with : can you do without the still benediction of the Father? Can you endure to have your life laid bare and not find in it one gentle or kindly deed to one of these least of the brethren of the Judge? Can you go on without listening to the voice within urging you on to light up these *little* acts with the ready will and devotion to God which makes of them the only deeds that will stand at that day when the fan shall winnow out from history the victories of warrior and statesman, and shrivel them into dust? If you can, you have a strong heart. ·

Lastly, mark the result. Peter bent himself to the duty which lay before him, and at whatever cost he finished it. All night he toiled, and unsuccessfully : His faith and his devotion were to be sorely tried. " And that night they caught nothing."

But with early morn a figure was seen on the shore. Ghostly, glimmering through the dawn it stood there, as though to mock at the fishers' bootless toil. The wearied disciples looked at it, but their eyes were holden that they should not see. At last a well-known voice addresses them—"Children." Still they are not sure. But the voice of love suggests, "It is the Lord." Then mindful of the respect due to the Master, Peter girds on him his fisher's coat, and heedless now of the dangers of the sea which had once shaken his faith, casts himself into the waters. At last the Saviour is here. Here, no longer to be doubted, appearing in the path of duty. Here, as the gentle Master who had long since rejected all harsher titles and adopted that of "Friends," and now calling them to a yet nearer relation as "Children." No wonder that at that endearing word Peter forgot his doubts and cast himself headlong into the sea. No wonder that he could not wait to clasp that loved one whom he had denied, and of whose forgiveness he yearned to be convinced,

So is it with every one who tries to find the Saviour in those scenes which He most loved to haunt—the uninviting round of duty. In vain will you seek him in the loftier sphere of longing ambition. Down, down amid those humble duties which you have forced upon you every day —there must you seek, if you would have your search crowned with success.

My hearer, has your life been shaken to its foundation by the loss of what seemed your life itself, and do you sit desolate among the ruins? Or has no touch from Heaven ever kindled a fire on the altar of your heart, and do you wait for your task to be forced upon you?

Go forth like Peter, and do what lies before you. Believe that when you have obeyed the voice which bids you do what you are unwilling to do—to enter on the discharge of duty which now is so distasteful, you will have taken the step that will make all other steps easy. Your toil will become light to you, for there is a wondrous power in the consciousness of doing our duty to make the rough places smooth.

And, as all good is linked together by adamantine chains, through the darkness of your soul will grow clearer and clearer the form of the Son of God. He seemed to leave you to yourself that He might try your faith : when it has come out of the ordeal unscathed, He will return to you, dearer than before, a thousand times dearer, because you will know that He looks lovingly upon you as a soldier who has fought well, as a servant who has done his duty, as a friend who has kept his friendship pure, as a child who may henceforth repose with fearless trust in His Father's bosom.

XIV.

CONFIRMATION.

SECOND SUNDAY AFTER TRINITY.

"O Lord who never failest to help and govern those whom Thou dost bring up in thy steadfast fear and love, keep us, we beseech Thee, under the protection of Thy good providence, and make us to have a perpetual fear and love of Thy holy name, through Jesus Christ our Lord."

THE Collect for the Second Sunday after Trinity will give the key-note of what I have to say. It seems to sum up the duties, and the support of all Christian lives so perfectly that it may with fitness guide our thoughts on an occasion like this. For to-day we have with us our Father in God, the Bishop, to whom, according to unbroken usage since the Apostles' days in the Catholic Church, it belongs regularly to admit to the highest privilege of Christians those who have determined to profess the faith of Christ crucified. About every occasion of this kind there is something which strongly impresses the imagination. The religious life, as I devoutly believe, has truly begun in the case of those whom we are to-day to welcome to a full participation in the privileges of members of the Christian Church. We do not reckon the ancient rite of confirmation as occupying in any sense the position of a sacrament. Grace, we hold, is not communicated in it in the same way as in baptism, and the Lord's Supper. It is not like them the outward and visible sign

167

of an inward and spiritual grace appointed by Christ Himself, but by His Apostles. But who can doubt that on such an occasion grace is divinely conveyed to all those who come forward with hearts full of repentance, of faith, of resolution henceforward to live such a life as is pictured to us in the words of the baptismal office? The very business, or one of the chief duties of the Christian Church is to save us from the vagueness and indecision which are found to infect the lives of those who presume to forsake the assembling of themselves together. We cannot live healthy, religious lives unless we give utterance to our religious hopes and desires, any more than a ship-wrecked man, who in his solitude never uses the divine gift of speech, can, when long years are passed, retain his power to utter the words of his mother tongue. Such a means of expressing before others, and to God, the deep-seated feelings connected with all true religion, the Church supplies. In the baptism of infants in public, how deeply is our belief strengthened in the undeserved and mysterious grace of God! In our devout reception of the Holy Communion, how do we gain year by year in our reliance upon the never-failing treasury of divine strength! In our ordinary gatherings for public worship is it not plain to us that the dew of God's blessing falls far more largely upon our weary hearts than it could were we presumptuously to shut ourselves off from the benefits of *public*, as distinguished from solitary, private prayer? So, too, in the solemn ceremony for which we are assembled. In the spectacle of immortal souls who have by God's grace been brought to feel the need of buckling on the Christian armor, in the sight of those to whom the promises of the Christian warfare are about to become the watchword of life, you will see the exhibition of the triumph of human strength aided by God, over the temptations of the World, the Flesh, and the Devil. Than that spectacle, earth has nothing which ought to be more inspiring. It is the expression in its noblest form of that which makes us differ from the brute. It is the well-weighed utterance of faith in the truth that Holiness is stronger than sin, and must be the final conqueror. It is the proclamation, not before those alone who gather in our little Church, but before the Church militant and the Church triumphant, before an innumerable company of angels, before God, the Judge of all, that these souls are ready, God being their helper, to defy the powers of darkness, and to make themselves an offering to Him. Compared with this, what other scene of life is so solemn, so absorbing in its interest? I know of none. Even that last scene of all, when our feet lose their hold on the familiar ground of earthly life, and we silently pass into the great unknown sea of being, even this derives, to Christian eyes, all its character from knowing whether or not the promise to be made to-day has been kept. As we accompany along their path of life these new soldiers of Christ, sorrow and joy, trial and recompense, health and sickness, all the manifold triumphs and reverses of human life, present themselves to the mind as full of terror, or full of peace, according as they are, or are not, in the spirit of obedience to the profession which shall be made before us to-day.

Taking then as our guide the beautiful collect I have read, let us try to gain some more clear notion of what the Christian life may be and ought to be. Let us not do this in a spirit of sentimental reverie, but as a very grave thing; not as though the most experienced Christian

8

among us had outgrown the need of having his aspirations raised, and his aims made more clear, but with the deep conviction that to old and young alike the great truths which make up our Christian life are ever in want of being quickened into fresh vigor, and made more strongly operative upon our daily existence.

Beginning with the first part of our Collect, can any of us say that his experience has not persuaded him of the necessity of learning over and over again the truth that God never fails to help and govern those whom He brings up in His steadfast fear and love ? That combination of fear and love—how hard is it to maintain! How peculiarly apt is the one of those feelings to encroach on the other ! Especially in this loose-thinking, sentimental age when men are given to fastening on some one portion of divine truth, and holding it to the exclusion of every other, we imperatively demand for our soul's health that humble reverence in our demeanor to God which is the soul of religion. On every side, I seem to see the working of this irreverent spirit. In every body of Christians, signs are not wanting that the rounded body of revealed truth in its unflinching utterance of the terrible along with the winning, in its unhesitating way of coupling the punishment of the unbeliever with the blessedness of the faithful, is looked upon, not as the august and severely beautiful temple built by God for the indwelling of the human soul, but rather as savages regard the ruins of ancient temples— a quarry whence men, unable to understand what they are destroying, may plunder materials for their own rude hovels. This I am sure is one of the crying evils of our times. There is indeed no lack of interest in matters religious, either at home or aboard. Half a century ago men would have laughed incredulously had the prophecy been ventured that the various subjects connected with religion would become a theme of interest so profound as that which to-day attends the host of books, pamphlets, and reviews which deal with them. It would then have seemed one of the wildest vagaries of the mind of man to suppose that religion, and the connection between Church and State, would so soon become the most critical of the questions agitating Europe. But all the more is it needful that Christians should be on their guard against the dangers with which such a period is rife. Much of what we see and hear, however closely it may be *connected* with Christianity is pervaded by a deeply unchristian spirit. It resembles the attempts which were made when Christianity first took before the Roman Empire the position which belongs to it—I mean the attempts to rob it of its foundation, to get the spirit of it apart from the revealed truths which beget the spirit, and try to be Christians without believing in Christ as the Son of God, and the Saviour of the world. So now, every one of us who reads or talks much on religious matters is sure to find the disposition to believe as much of Christianity as suits the taste, and to reject the rest. What is Unitarianism but this, under whatever name it disguises itself? We have around us far too much warning, to allow us any excuse if we venture thus to trifle with revealed truths. And since there are many specious kinds of this disbelief, and many bewildering varieties in the expression of it, we should strive to make it our principle in living Christian lives, to keep ourselves in such steadfast fear and love of the great Teacher of our souls, as may fill us with an awful dread of casting away any part of the lesson He has set for us to learn. We should ask Him to teach us so perfectly to trust His love that we may be content to leave for Him to settle all the dark questions that sometimes tempt us to press in with our puny fancies upon the mysterious ground where God alone can safely tread. You think that this is too hard a thing to do? You say to yourself that when you think on such solemn subjects as conversion, and predestination, and eternal death, you must trust to your own conclusions no matter what may be the consequences? True as this is in one sense, in another it betrays just the lack of fear and love which I have warned you against. Those questions have been discussed in many centuries, and the results have always been disastrous just in proportion to the irreverent self-reliance which has been displayed. Take, for instance, that profoundly mysterious subject of predestination. One of the most powerful minds of the Reformation undertook to settle it, to map out with distinctness the whole subject; and what was the consequence? Look at New England, and you can answer. The terrible consequences of this system of belief are apparent in the total rejection of Christianity, by men to whom Christianity meant distinctly that from all eternity God had predestinated souls to eternal death, and that Christ died only for a limited number of the elect. Far be it from me to say how much truth, and how much untruth there may be in the system of Calvin. Far be it from me to say that there is not a vast number of noble Christians among those who believe, or think they believe, it all. I only say that it is one of those subjects about which we should be most reverent in our thinking, — that we need in regard to it peculiarly to exercise together the fear and love which belong to the wise

Christian, that our speculations concerning it are specially apt to land us in a state where our fear will be supplanted by irreverence, and our love by a feeling which makes it impossible for us heartily to cry, Abba Father!

But still you ask how am I to avoid thinking on subjects like these, and how am I to know when I have thought enough? Is it not asking me to do that which we so much object to in the Romish system, to submit myself to the decisions of an infallible Church, and believe what, not a Priest indeed, but a book of articles bids me believe? I fully admit the difficulty of this question. It is one to which no universally applicable reply can be made. But it is one which in religious matters answers itself, just as similar questions answer themselves in common life. Is it likely that you will ever come to regard suicide as a praiseworthy act? If not, why not? You may, if you choose, reflect on the matter—you may look upon it in all its lights—you may contemplate all the advantages likely to flow from a man's ridding himself of the pains of incurable disease, or the anguish of irremediable disgrace. Men do, or pretend that they do, see that, on the whole, suicide is sometimes a very noble and admirable way of terminating one's career. Do you feel any apprehension that your reflections will ever lead you to cut your throat? We have all, I suppose. had the notion flit across our minds in seasons of acute, bodily, or mental anguish. But do you feel the slightest danger that in your own case you will ever be led to the crime? The reason is a very simple one. The natural, instinctive love of life has been so fortified by our training, that we do not allow our thoughts on the subject to go beyond a certain, curious speculation. We are not conscious of peremptorily cutting short our thoughts about it, but the result is just the same as though we did. In that respect, we Americans, in general, at least, are in no danger so long as our minds remain in their proper balance. And yet, from causes opposed to this, among foreigners of some nationalities it is not uncommon.

Apply this, which I do not select at random, to the religious life. No man who has at all understood what Christianity and Christ are, *can* deliberately discuss with himself the question whether he shall or shall not continue to believe in God. There may be moments when one whom duty forces to consider the attacks of unbelief, or more often in the case of one who has dallied with infidelity out of mere idle curiosity, when such an one feels himself tempted to doubt of everything. But the question must have been pretty well settled already, when one allows one's self to discuss the matter deliberately and coolly. For to give up one's faith in God means to commit suicide of the soul, so far as that is within our power. In the great number of Christians, even among those who think much about these deep matters, the danger of such an act depends upon the closeness or slackness of the union and intercourse which is kept up with God—in the words of our Collect, upon our steadfast or our wavering fear and love. Only when we have grown cold in devotion, only when we have suffered the cloud of indifference to gather between us and God are we in any peril. That which is true of total abandonment of faith is true likewise regarding those partial desertions of the truth of Christianity of which I have spoken.

God never fails to help and govern those who allow Him to bring them up in steadfast fear and love. Trace back any one dark period of your religious life to its origin, and you will find that it is due to the wilful abandonment of His governance over you—to your letting lower motives sway you, such as cowardice or indolence, or what is called in Scripture the spirit of the world. Here it is—here, and not in any forcible choking down of our liberty of think- ing, that we find the safeguard against letting go the faith. The daily growth of the soul in grace lets in gleam after gleam of light upon the questions which otherwise are so apt to puzzle us. You do not consciously say, I will not think upon this or that dark question; you are penetrated more and more deeply with the feeling that there are heights and deeps of spiritual truth which can be disclosed to your strengthening eyesight only little by little. You cannot put into definite words your growing feeling about predestination, or the atonement, or the workings of divine grace. But you are less and less tempted, and why? be- cause with the increasing sense of His help and govern- ance, there comes the feeling that sublime mysteries like these are not capable of being put into the meagre forms of human speech. They become, not dry, colorless beliefs, but convictions—as little expressible in the fullness of their heavenly light and meaning, as is your affection to your child when he asks you how much you love him, as though the multiplication table were amply sufficient to tell it all.

I seem perhaps to have made as far too much of our Christian beliefs as I have said the disposition is to make too little. But the truth is, belief and life are only two expressions, inward and outward, of one and the same thing. Belief is impossible in its only valuable meanings without a corresponding life: life needs belief to shape and guide it. I do not say merely that one is worthless in the total absence of the other. It cannot *be*.

When you feel that your Christian life is at its best, you may, if you choose, feel its intimate connection with the belief, as the highest state of bodily health does not do away with the functions of the heart and lungs, but depends on their proper discharge. Unless you put your hand upon your heart you may forget that you have one but if it be disordered, a very slight amount of exertion tells you unmistakably of its diseased state. From the similar relation of belief to spiritual life it comes, that in all ages that have been distinguished by active religious vitality, so much stress has been laid upon correctness of faith, or to use a word which seems just now to be in rather bad odor, upon orthodoxy. And it needs but very little inspection to see that where orthodoxy is most decried, there is generally to be found a corresponding indifference to the sublimest privileges of religion. Personal piety, charity, genuine delight in prayer, in personal efforts for the instruction and bodily comfort of the destitute, faith, humble submission to God's dispensations, and the general and evident moulding of the life by heavenly motives,—I ask any one whether these are found most among those who reverently believe in all the doctrines of the Church, or among those who are in the habit of talking as though orthodoxy were rather another word for narrow-mindedness. If such a connection were really to be between the welcoming of all that God has revealed and a working out of all that He has commanded, I need no further grounds for my urging both on those who are Churchmen already, and on those who are to-day to be admitted to the Church's highest privileges, the solemn duty of so fearing God as to receive with devout awe His disclosures of Himself, and so loving Him, as to trust in His hands the wise and merciful deciding of questions too hard for us to settle. The Collect closes with a petition that we may be kept under the *protection* of His good Providence. For twelve hundred years at least, this prayer has gone up from mouths of Christians. During the darkest periods of the Church's history—amid persecution and warfare, in private doubt, in trial, in anxiety, it has resounded under the arches of old Cathedrals as it resounds now in the huts which serve to shelter God's people in the western wilds. Can we not picture to ourselves the peace which for all these centuries has been imparted by the view of life given us in that one word, protection? Surely the holy man who penned it first, must have been one who after toil and storm at length had reached a purer air. Who can estimate the experience of him whose instinctive way of thinking about Providence, was not of a succession of trials and discipline, sorely taxing strength and faith, but rather a divinely wrought shield, sheltering God's chosen, and only nourishing to fuller life the love and fear of His holy name?

The finest bloom and fragrance of the human soul went, one cannot doubt, to the composition of this exquisite prayer. How can one ever sufficiently thank the Church's Head and Master, for inspiring and preserving these choicest utterances of His saints throughout centuries! And yet amidst the thanksgivings which we raise to Him for our Liturgy, let us never forget our own higher obligations to preserve and show forth as the result of His dealings with the Church, a piety which shall be worthy of such prayers. That alone is worthy of him who has learned by heart the difficult lesson set before us in the use of the words to which I have just called your attention. It is the most appropriate lesson with which to end an address to persons beginning the professed Christian life—that of so ordering our lives that we may have this as the unshakable foundation for them,—that God's Providence is one of protection. So will it always manifest itself to him, who will make the fear and love of God's holy name his constant companions.

All the changes and chances of this mortal life are to him, but manifestations of God's abounding love. All the calamities which human life brings with it, are changed by that habitual temper into loving discipline. He learns to sun himself in the light of that eternal judgment which in Scripture is so nobly displayed to us as but the unchanging manifestation of God's truthfulness. And thus strengthened, and purified, and protected by His good Providence, he so passes through things temporal that he finally loses not the things eternal. May this day be such a beginning of endless life to those who are to join us in fighting the good fight of faith.

XV.

CHARITY AND ITS ABUSES.

I SUPPOSE that no reflecting person can doubt, that we are in this part of the country doing all we can to create a real class of paupers—of professional beggars, unwilling to work, spending the pleasanter part of the year in prowling through the land, and in winter leading lives of crime at large or of indolence in the poor-houses. Those who regard the matter with attention proportioned to the magnitude of the evil, are beginning to feel that some organized means must be adopted for the purpose of destroying a disease shown by the experience of other countries to be full of danger to society at large, and of incalculable injury to the persons who are continually tempted to enroll themselves for life in this ragged army of criminals. Attempts have been made here and there, to deal with the evil by law, and to authorize the arrest and confinement at hard labor, of persons found wandering through the country, with no better means of livelihood than beggary. Such interference with liberty, running, as it does, the risk of unjustly confining persons travelling on foot for the most worthy purposes, cannot, of course, be defended in this shape. Perhaps no legal measures can be expected ever adequately to deal with the evil. And it certainly is not with the object of suggesting anything of that description that I introduce the subject now; but rather that we may consider together some of its aspects as they concern our-

179

selves as individuals and as Christians, the duty incumbent upon us in that capacity, the discouragements perpetually arising in connection with its discharge, and what we have, and have not, the right to look for, in due compliance with Christ's commands regarding the relief of human want.

It must be apparent that in a country like our own, under ordinary circumstances, there can be no good reason why a *class* of beggars should exist. Exceptional cases, of course, there will always be—cases where temporary sickness, or the death of the father of a family may justify an appeal for relief until the first stress of want is passed, or, even permanently, where health is hopelessly gone, and the only alternative is starvation or the poor-house. But these are exceptions. The evil I speak of is of much larger proportions—proportions with which we are every day made familiar. It offers itself, perhaps more strikingly during a period of business depression, but not so very much more than in the years of unhealthy prosperity, under the form of numbers of strong men presenting themselves for relief, and relief in the shape of money. Those who have paid personal attention to such appeals are aware that year after year the same individuals in groups easily recognizable, present themselves at certain seasons, always with much the same piteous tale. These persons become professional vagabonds during the warmer months, encamping in the woods and levying tribute upon the decent classes of society by begging and stealing, or in colder weather, by burglary. Now such a state of things may seem to one nothing worse than annoying, and hardly worth bestowing upon it more than a passing regret. But it is by neglecting the rise of such a social phenomenon, and by treating the evil improperly, that in European countries has been formed a pauper class, handing down from father to son those habits of depredation and dependence, with the principle of self-respect utterly killed out of them, and, in the course of generations, becoming almost incapable of being raised from their condition of hostility to all the restraints necessary to make up human society. It is such a class which, when congregated in a city, always furnishes by far the largest portion of the mobs that destroy life and property, and jeopard the best interests of the community. It is such outcasts who made up, largely, the insurgents of Paris in the first Revolution, and during the late reign of the Commune. And, as I began by remarking, instead of wisely-concerted measures for checking its growth, we are weakly fostering it as far as negligence, and culpable laxity in giving can do so.

Looking at the matter from this point of view, can any one say that the subject is not of the gravest practical moment, whether regarded with the eyes of a statesman, a philanthropist, or a lover of his country. And no less grave than the evil is the responsibility of those who unthinkingly aggravate it. If we are so acting as to stimulate the growth of such a social disease, we surely need only to become aware of it in order to feel that we are bound to reconsider our course, and to adopt one that shall benefit the objects of our charity, but at the same time be a true carrying out of our Lord's loving commands.

For after all, this last consideration, in this place, and to those who come here for sincerely religious purposes, must be the most important of all to settle. Incalculable as is the importance of other objects affected by this question—valuable as are the interests of society—we should feel that the true following out of Christ's bidding must be in itself more so still. We might be led by looking *merely* at the social side of the matter to the conclusion, so heartlessly avowed by some, that the interests of society on the whole are best served by refusing all relief, under all circumstances, and leaving the world to be freed by death from persons whose condition shows them to be useless to advance its welfare; and yet, however swayed his mind might be by presentation of such a doctrine, every Christian would feel that there must be some fatal mistake in a course of reasoning so completely opposed to the utterances of the Son of God.

Let us then, having begun by thinking of its worst form, seek for the fountain-head of this alarming evil, and try to shape to ourselves a consistent notion of what our course should be. For harm may be done, not simply when dealing with that peculiarly dangerous, and one might almost say, organized body of mendicants of whom I began by speaking, but also when ministering to the needs of others, so far much superior to them. We may, by rightly graduating and adapting our charities, make a means of religious influence of a high order, or by thoughtlessness, impair the spirit of self-dependence, without which, it is hardly too much to say, no fine, or Christian character can exist; and thus even prepare those whom we mean to benefit for enrolling themselves in that very host of professional beggars whose dangers I have pointed out.

The main point for us to settle is whether private, individual alms-giving is a permissible form for our charity to take; and if so, what shape it should assume. By permissible, of course, I mean, calculated to do lasting and real good. And much is here to be said on both sides. Unquestionably such action is exposed to considerable danger of the kind just referred to. No one much acquainted with such matters need be told of the vast amount of imposture that finds in private charity a soil in which it thrives luxuriantly. Appeals to various individuals at the same time, and the receipt of aid from each, frequently make pretended poverty the means of getting a comfortable livelihood. When again, the giver's feelings are not controlled by judgment, the motive to exertion on the part of the person relieved is often weakened and at last completely killed. Both of these are instances from which it might seem proper to conclude that the best way of giving would be to put one's alms into the hands of some person or persons whose special business it should be to investigate each case as it arises, and who from occupying this position would be guarded by a feeling of responsibility from excessive giving. And in the city, I doubt not, very largely, and to a considerable degree in the country, this is a proper course to pursue. But to resort to it wholly is a plan open to very serious objections. One of the greatest uses of charity is that it creates, when properly conducted, a bond of true sympathy between the giver and the person relieved which is admirable in its effects on both. One who visits and relieves the fatherless and the widow in their affliction is greatly helped thereby in obedience to the injunction that follows—to keep himself unspotted from the world. The sight of human suffering, looked at with a Christian eye, helps one better to estimate the difficulties with which a large proportion of mankind, in one form or another, have to struggle. It deepens one's sense of unworthiness; it can hardly fail to check selfishness, and abate the disposi-

tion to personal indulgence which is one of the most dis-
quieting symptoms of our times. When suffering is
patiently and manfully borne, it supplies us with examples
the most eloquent to help us in conquering discontent
and cultivating a deep and cheerful spirit of piety. And
for the benefit of the sufferer it is of untold value. The
official almoner or dispenser of other's charities, however
sympathizing he may be, or however generous in quietly
giving of his own means, will lose with many, at least
something of his due influence from being in that position.
The most valuable means of improving both yourself
and those whom you would benefit is to see and know
them yourself; to have, and to manifest a personal interest
in their welfare. This will give you the opening for advice, for consolation, for enlightening ignorance, and im-
parting those large and elevated views of Christianity
which do not come in general under such circumstances,
save from the outside—from persons whose superior knowledge has enabled them to divine the truth about many
matters which to ignorance are dark and burdensome.

There is another reason too, which makes of this form
of charity a peculiarly valuable means of furthering our
own spiritual growth. You remember, how after his ship-
wreck on the island of Melita, while the shivering crew
and the inhabitants of the isle were kindling a fire, St.
Paul while working with them was bitten by a viper and
was expected to fall dead. Some similar recompense of
our Christian activity we often meet with, and in it lies
one of the chief advantages of this course of discipline
which I have called private charity. When one has
practised it, it often becomes so attractive that we are in
danger of forgetting the lofty end which is its chief rea-

son, and sometimes even lose sight of other duties in the pleasure afforded by the discharge of this. Some of the most telling, and yet most truthful of the pictures of a famous novelist are those which delineate the spiritual pride or the utter neglect of the most sacred duties sometimes resulting from excessive abandonment to philanthropic or charitable work. Every one is familiar with the feeling produced by meeting with ingratitude and selfishness, or worse, among those who have been carefully and kindly treated—the feeling almost of personal affliction engendered by the discovery of one's utter deception in a character hitherto held in affectionate esteem. Painful as this is when one's efforts have been distinctly and really made from a feeling of duty, and when pleasure has not been aimed at by itself, the shock is greater yet when the latter has unconsciously thrust itself forward, and we have been blindly following our own impulses. It is under these circumstances that most harm is done. The gratification of a generous nature is so great when suffering is relieved, that unless checked by a very stern sense of responsibility, it is very apt indeed to lead to such a liberality as produces the consequences before adverted to as harmful in a high degree. And not merely material gifts are liable to do this evil. The unregulated feelings are, if possible, still more liable to mislead, when, not food and clothing, and the outward necessaries of life, but comfort and sympathy are given to those who really need, for their own good, wholesome rebuke, or warning against discontent, or lessons of frugality from neglect of which their trouble comes. In this way, instead of doing good, we may be encouraging the grossest forms of spiritual disease,—pride, ingratitude, a disposition to grumble at not being as well-to-do as is wished, and particularly, the fatal vice of hypocrisy, pretending to high spiritual attainments when, in reality, there is not even common morality to be found. Every one, I say, is more or less familiar with this experience; and, as matters stand with us, painful as it is, perhaps it is needed from time to time in order to remind us of the real nature and ground of the duty in whose discharge we encounter it, and particularly, to enforce the need of that rigid inspection of our methods without which we are so likely to do more harm than good. As to the former point, certainly, here as elsewhere, pleasure very pure and great is conjoined with the proper discharge of duty. But when pleasure, consciously or unconsciously, assumes too much importance, it is apt to prevent, and finally to destroy, the usefulness of our efforts thus tainted by selfishness. This displays itself in quarters the most unlooked for. Self-denial, that is in its severer forms, yields high and serene pleasure; but do we not know how often it leads to spiritual pride—how even religious exercises, practised to the neglect of less delightsome duties, make us uncharitable, and inclined to underrate the godliness of others? So here. Instances are not unknown where utter devotion to a charitable work, accompanied by an undue pride in it, has rendered an active philanthropist blind not only to Christian kindness but even to the ordinary proprieties of life. Such cases, of course, are rare, but probably, rare only because the pleasure derived from such activities has not been suffered to grow too important an object. Wherever though, this does take place, to even a slight degree, there is the need of disappointments to disturb our self-satisfaction and bend our attention once more to the true object and plan of the duty.

When thus violently and painfully aroused to the mistakes we have made, we naturally turn to the task of providing against them for the future. We remember that the great purpose should be, not merely, and for itself, making people happy and comfortable, for the time being, but so relieving them as to work lasting good to their characters. That great army of idle vagabonds which we considered at the outset, are seen, under the light of such experiences as these, to be but the natural and inevitable outgrowth of unthinking and ill-regulated private charity. If we try only to relieve temporary want we lay the foundation of that superstructure of delusions which finds its logical result in Communism—the belief that, independently of his own qualifications, his character, his industry, his thrift, every man has a *right* to be supported in comfort:—to sum up in a word, that in the phrase of Proudhon, "private property is itself robbery." As a matter of fact, I have little or no doubt that our professional vagrants have reached their present numbers from finding it easier to beg or steal than to work, and for them vastly more comfortable; and that they are the offspring, largely, of persons whose self-respect has been destroyed in the same way. Whether this be so or not, however, it is manifest that instead of diminishing, this dangerous and wretched class will increase, if the causes producing it go on unchecked. Let us look to our methods and see if they cannot be mended.

As regards the vagrant class our duty is pretty clear. On the whole perhaps, we do much harm by supplying even with food a class which is led to spend half the year in vagrancy by knowing that it can obtain regular nourishment. And yet there is the risk of perhaps denying to a really needy person food that is necessary for the support of life; and with proper vigilance that our bounty is not thrown away, we may feel safe in obeying this instinct of the heart. As for any money assistance it is, under almost all circumstances, likely to do harm to persons of this class. Money so procured is used in most cases for the worst purposes, and to give it is a direct encouragement to indolence and to vice. Now and then, of course, a case will present itself where you may venture to believe the piteous story told you, and act accordingly; but in general, every one should feel that by giving money to unknown beggars, he is not merely wasting it but committing a crime against society, and fostering the growth of a class of persons whose existence is a standing menace against it. Ask yourself for an instant what means may be looked to for the conversion into decent members of society of these stalwart beggars, for their learning habits of industry and thrift, for their becoming amenable to any elevating influences. It is plain that regular settled habitations are almost the first necessary thing in the process, then, enforced self-support. Enforce it we cannot directly, but we may indirectly, by rendering it impossible, so far as we are concerned, to obtain a living by merely asking for it. When once it shall be plain to this wretched and at present, hopelessly degraded class, that their present means of existence will no longer suffice, they will do one of two things:—they will plunder openly or they will work. And observe this: always it has turned out that if they were not thus forced to support themselves when comparatively few in numbers, they have proved impossible to control after growing stronger. We have dealt too loosely with a serious social danger. It is our bounden duty to dally with it no longer, but to treat it on principle, systematically, because we thereby best follow the spirit of Christ's own bidding. And when we have thus convinced ourselves of the seriousness of the evil, we shall be prepared to understand, and intelligently to support, whatever public measures may be proposed. First of all however, must be private conviction, and loyalty to it.

As for the methods according to which we are to conduct our ordinary charities towards persons whom we know, the pointing out of the evils flowing from the wrong course will naturally suggest them. The first thing to be settled, I presume, must be a strong desire for the lasting good of the person relieved. Now trouble, we know, is nothing but one form of divine discipline, and it is always to be remembered in the discharge of this duty that we are doing wrong and harm, not good, by encouraging in any way the spirit of discontent to which such discipline commonly gives rise. A provision of the necessaries of life, and yet the most careful training of whatever desire for self-support may exist; a most jealous and watchful care that that back-bone of character, self-respect, be not weakened; eagerness rather to see habits and faculties of mind and body acquired for future use, than simply to relieve passing wants of the body;—these should be the general type according to which we should do our part as stewards of the manifold blessings of God.

On account of both giver and receiver, there must be watchfulness on the benefactor's part that his feelings do not carry him into a misunderstanding of the facts of the case. In many of the instances, especially in a great city, where relief is needed, the character has already sunk under some of the manifold evil influences of the situation.

Very often indeed, faults of the meanest kind have flourished under the fostering influence of continuous dependence on others for support. We are guilty, then, of the most short-sighted folly when we allow ourselves to look among such for the return it would be reasonable to anticipate from others. As a general rule, to which, however, I am glad to remember some exceptions, you are utterly to abandon the thought of gratitude for what you do, as a physician never expects a child to understand how much has been done for it. This is an important thing to bear in mind. Otherwise we are so sickened and disheartened by the discovery of baseness and thanklessness, that we are almost inclined to give up a duty, which however little return it may have in outward gratification, is still a duty imposed upon us by God, and as impossible to deny as that which demands obedience from child to parent. And moreover, too lofty an estimate will seriously impede us in the use of those moral means which the position of benefactor usually puts at one's disposal. Generally speaking, continuous want springs from thriftlessness, extravagance, foolish pride, and a false notion of the degradation caused by any honest labor. These are grave faults, and it is every benefactor's bounden duty to discourage and check them. Every thing likely to blind us to the existence of such faults then, is so much in the way of our rightly using the means of doing good. We must see clearly in order to act wisely.

I have treated this subject because I believe it to be of vast importance from whatever point of view regarded. I have attempted to arouse no specially poetical or romantic notions regarding it, but rather to suggest the need of turning the immense amounts which annually go to support these public pests and enemies into the channel indicated by reflection and true philanthropy. The relief of want is not a duty which can be successfully discharged without grave thought and a feeling of responsibility. It is never so imperfectly done as when we look to it merely for pleasurable excitement.

> " God will not let love's work impart
> Full solace, lest it steal the heart."

The true spirit in which to perform it is that in which we come to the Holy Communion—the sense of unworthiness, of weakness, of the need of spiritual help, of gratitude to God for the gift of His dear Son, and the feeling that, being redeemed by Him, all men are our brothers. Thus feeling, we shall not be overmuch cast down by disappointments that are inevitable. And thus strong in our faith, we shall look to Him unceasingly for help in carrying on the work to which His earthly life was devoted, that through our patience and long-suffering, the weary and heavy-laden may come unto Him and find rest.

XVI.

THE POWER OF AN ENDLESS LIFE.

" The power of an endless life."—HEB. vii. 16.

WHO can survey the broadest expanse of principle, and from that vantage-ground discern the most accurately the far-reaching results of the agencies around them? Are they not those who are in other respects the noblest—whose lives are animated by the truest principles—whose souls are ever straining after the best ends?

So, on the other hand, if we begin with the latter consideration, we shall find that this nobility of soul—the aspiration after such ends, is joined with the *power* of surveying the most extensive fields of inquiry or of action.

This invariable connection of greatness of soul with the entertainment of broad views, cannot be accidental. What is the reason? Is it true that these men are *born* to such a heritage, and that no others can gain it? Or is it not rather that the constant contemplation of high destinies, itself exerts an ennobling influence upon the mind?

Whatever amount of truth there may be in the former supposition—however it may be that some men enter by right of birth upon the enjoyment of this grand heritage, the truth of the latter statement is more unquestionable still. Men *can* be raised by the habitual contemplation of great truths and high destinies to a pitch of greatness never dreamed of before.

Look at the world around you and see why the majori-

192

ty of those who compose it lead such lives. It is because they have no appreciation of anything beyond the lowest motives. To amass money and to acquire thereby consideration in society—to gratify their tastes and enjoy themselves,—are not these the aims of the great proportion of mankind? They live only from day to day: or if the future exerts any influence over them, it is a very limited future that they look forward to, and the vista that stretches before them is not one that reveals ends of a lofty character. Practically, the power of an endless life has no place among the influences which sway them.

Suppose society at large, however, aroused from this condition. Suppose the truth that we are immortal beings to become an ever-present thought,—pervading every department of life,—influencing every branch of activity. Let the thought that we are pursuing a career which is never to end, and each of whose successive stages is moulded by that which went before, be an hourly companion. Can you help seeing how elevating it would be? Beneath the over-shadowing majesty of a conviction like this, the paltry cares and ambitions that fill our day would cower into nothingness, awed out of existence. Drawn onward with irresistible force along the ever-widening avenue of an endless life, men would grow, not simply able to resist, but incapable of bestowing engrossing thought upon those things that now exert so disturbing an influence. So mighty a belief must expand the soul in which it abides. It must crowd out the mean and paltry, and assimilate to itself the whole man. But this is only the general statement of a felt immortality. Let us see more exactly how it will operate.

Nothing great can be done by little men, or by men

9

who feel themselves little. However grieved by his short-comings, or humiliated by his sins, the man who does great deeds must know that he has in himself something that links him to their grandeur. Nay, even this repentance, this humiliation, are they not themselves the proof that he does not deem himself wholly base? It is just because he feels sin to be a surrender of his high destiny —a practical dishonoring of himself—a falling short of the lofty part which God gave him to enact, that his remorse is so bitter. It is because he knows that by admitting him to communion with Himself, by breathing the Holy Spirit into his heart, God gave him the assurance of a holy and hence a noble life. This feeling, which, for want of a better name, must be called pride, is essential to the achievement of lofty deeds. Only let it be remembered that it is a feeling as far removed from vanity or self-glorification as Heaven is from earth. It is ever joined with the truest humility. Its possessor reverently bows before God as the source of all his endowments. He aspires after greatness, not as a means of gaining applause, but as the only thing possible for a soul which comes from God, and which was created to love and glorify and serve its Maker.

Now that which the Epistle to the Hebrews calls the power of an endless life, nourishes a feeling of this description—it must give rise to the sentiment of moral dignity that we see to be so essential to any nobility of action.

So long as men live practically as though their life were as brief as that of the beasts that perish—so long as their desires are bounded by the satisfying of wants that belong only to earth, their endless life puts forth none of its power. For any influence it has upon them, what they act upon might as well be true—they might as well have had no higher destiny than the insect which flutters from morn to eve amid the glories of a summer's day. Thinking themselves little, they become so in reality. Alive to none of their capacities, they lose those capacities. As they become more and more wrapt up in unworthy pursuits, their souls shrink to the measure of the thoughts and principles that govern them.

But upon a soul thus doing dishonor to its capabilities, imagine the effect, when into its narrow work-house breaks the consciousness of that life and immortality which Christ brought to light by the Gospel! We saw before, in general, how ennobling will be the effect of such a discovery. Now, guided by the thought of the necessity of a sense of greatness to the performance of great deeds, we can see more exactly *how* this change will be effected. The mist of uncertainty, or darkness, which once rested a few steps before the man, rendering him incapable of planning for more than a few days, or months, or years, suddenly lifts, and he beholds, stretching far on into infinity the path which seemed so short. He feels that all along that road, he will be accompanied by the influences of each deed that he is performing to-day; the good actions supporting him and cheering him to renewed exertions, the bad changing themselves into phantoms of malignant power to drag him aside. Can he, think you,—can he be again the little, pitiable thing he was before? Can he remain content with the trifles which were suited to the creature whose life was a span, when all his eternity opens before him? The stupendous part he is called to perform—the mighty sphere he is destined to fill—these arouse all the slumbering good in him, shame the pettiness into its proper insignificance, and spur him on to make himself worthy of God who admitted him to such privileges, of the Saviour who died to free him from his sins, of the Holy Ghost whose aid he must claim with each step toward the realization of those mighty hopes that have made him once more a man.

The reflections arising from such a discovery are so intimately linked together that they seem rather parts of one great whole than separate influences. But each of them exerts its own proper force. Thus as he feels day by day more keenly the magnitude of the future life, his yearning to fill it in a manner worthy of his high calling will be strengthened by finding that it is not a distinct, separate thing—this future existence—not one which is marked off by a clear line from the life he is living now, but simply a continuation of it. The boy looks forward wistfully to his manhood, and can hardly believe but that when he enters on what seem its unmingled delights, he shall undergo some instantaneous, radical change from his present self. The child, he thinks, busy with his ball and his marbles must disappear suddenly, or else he never can become like these men whom he hopes one day to resemble. But as the man looks back on the slow stages which have brought him on his way to maturity he sees no such sudden transformation. In their due time, the childish fancies and tastes which once occupied him melted away without his knowing it until they were gone, and in their stead, silently, mysteriously, arose others, of whose growth he was almost as unconscious, until one day he found himself to his surprise, what he had perhaps a year before been looking forward to as a far-off thing—a man. The gentle undulations in the path from infancy to maturity which to a little child, straining himself to look down into their depths, seemed mysterious abysses through which he could never pass without a sudden change, from the higher ground of manhood can hardly be distinguished in the unbroken highway which has led him on to his present standing-point.

Thus of earthly life and eternity. A change—a mighty change no doubt there is, between being a dweller on earth occupied exclusively with its concerns, and being *fit* for Heaven. But the mere passage across the dark river is not always the occasion of that change. Indeed it is very seldom so. The transformation must, almost always, take place long before.

For we must get rid of the almost materialistic thought that Heaven is something radically different from what it is possible to experience here. Since the soul is not to become infinite it must, after it enters upon the enjoyment of Heaven, be in some place; though the Bible has wisely refrained from dwelling too minutely upon such points as this. But the crowning bliss of that condition will undoubtedly be the communion with God that we shall enjoy. Now this is just what may be gained with increasing certainty and fulness on this side the tomb. Who does not know of Christians whose connection with this world is but as some gossamer thread, hardly felt, except as hindering them from actually quitting it, but whose souls are in constant intercourse with Him in whom they delight?

No, believe me, Heaven may begin on earth. It is a mighty revelation when we

" In one rapt moment know,
'Tis Heaven must come, not we must go."

The leaving of the scene of mortal pilgrimage is a thing

of but small moment to one, all of whose treasure has long since been laid up where neither moth nor rust doth corrupt, and where thieves do not break through nor steal. To be quit of the dangers of earth—of its cares and its toils—this no doubt, is a thing to be desired; but to such souls it grows plain, long before the summons comes, that that which makes Heaven is not denied even here, to him who by patient continuance in well-doing seeks for it. Let this become clear to any one, even though he be not fully up to so lofty a level, and see how it must affect him to think that earthly life is only the beginning of a pathway which even death overshadows but for a moment.

It will be much as when some little, turbulent, ill-governed province is made a part of a neighboring empire, vast in extent, moving harmoniously on to its destiny, under influences of law and order. The denizen of such a little province was, before, incapable of any thing grander· than some partizan fanaticism, because his mind was cramped by the petty limits within which alone he could call himself a citizen. The broils that agitated his neighborhood—the insignificant questions of its finance and trade occupied him exclusively. His province could not by any possibility gain a commanding position among the nations of the earth, and so its citizen, like its government, was denied the privilege of moving on a lofty course. But when to his rights as a dweller in that little section are superadded those of a member of a spreading empire, his thoughts and aspirations are correspondingly enlarged. The paltry cares and disputes and agitations of his community are stilled by the transition to a broader political life. The drop of water cast into the ocean is no longer conscious of its separate individual existence; it rises and falls with the wider and freer heaving of the tide that swells the grander body of which it has become a part.

And so with this earthly life of ours. How can I, with a sense of the magnitude of eternity upon me—flooded with the influence of its grandeur—how can I longer be willing to make this world the limit of my exertions? Engrafted into the commonwealth of Heaven, how can I think exclusively of my bodily cares and wants, content to fit myself to be forever an inhabitant of earth's narrow boundaries when those boundaries have disappeared, when it is merged into a domain as broad as infinity, and as imperial in its sway as the God who rules it? No, truly! As the anarchy and confusion around me sicken my heart, I will take to myself wings as a dove, I will flee away and be at rest in the longing anticipation of Heaven. And as the knowledge that I need not wait for Heaven to come to me at the hour of death becomes plain, the coarse prison-house around me will fade away, and in the discharge of its duties I shall feel that I am no more a bondsman chained to his task, but a cunning craftsman, fashioning to myself out of the materials around me,—the temptations and trials of the world,—a heaven that no tempest can overthrow. From the eternity of which I now feel that each day forms a part, will flow powers of law and order, stilling the turmoil which rages where eternity is lost from sight. Firm in my allegiance to the ruler of that august monarchy of which I am now a citizen, the distracting claims of inclination and unbridled license will be absorbed: inclination will incline to God, and license will be merged into the glorious liberty of His dear child. I have tasted of the powers of the world to come, and my lower appetites are dead.

No truth which is worth much to us but can be translated into the language of our daily life. Let it be as grand as it may when looked upon from a distance, it must be capable of being brought to bear upon the spiritual life. It is no argument against the value of a doctrine that you find a difficulty in so making use of it, for it may be on account of your own deficiencies; but what is in itself incapable of use is not a doctrine of very much importance.

I see, for example, how full of *daily* value are the fundamental truths of our religion. The Incarnation, teaching us that if Christ was willing to become man, our salvation is of untold moment in His eyes, and should be so in ours. The Atonement, giving us daily proof that through Him we have the way of access to God without which we are lost. The doctrine of the Spirit's power and operations, affording us in our loneliest hours, and in our deepest sorrows, the consolation that though deserted by human friends, a dearer friend than they shelters us under the shadow of His wing. Even the mysterious doctrine of the Trinity, at first sight so barren of use in our daily walk, but in whose absence our Saviour would be but a mere creature, not God—the Holy Ghost, only an influence—not the ever-present and all-powerful Person that we know Him to be.

So, too, if there be such a thing as an endless life, it will have a *power* belonging to it, and one which may be exerted not simply at some moment of respite from toil, when we are free to meditate on heavenly things, but even amid the smaller duties of civil or domestic life.

See how it will fare with you. The comparatively low motives which must influence one who has no ever-present

sense of the power of an endless life, die of inanition in
the atmosphere of eternity.   As such a man goes to his
daily toil, he is conscious that what he is toiling for is
something which is not to be estimated in earthly rewards
(which are the money of the worldling, but only the coun-
ters of the wise).   He cannot content himself at the year's
end by thinking that he has gained the dross after which
others strive.   There must have been acquisitions of a
nobler kind to satisfy him.   His *soul* must have won new
powers—he must have become wiser, better, more keen-
sighted to pierce the mists of time and see with increasing
certainty the rewards which this world can neither give
nor take away, but for which it is the appointed place in
which to strive.   Of what satisfying power to him are the
meeds from social consideration, unless along with these
he knows that he has increased in favor with his God.   To
what purpose is it that he has much goods laid up for
many years if he have bought them by starving the soul
from its due—if its powers have been bartered for things
which are in themselves powerless to minister to its needs?
Happy indeed is he, if he may gain both these ends, but
if only one of them can be his, the power of an endless
life, moulding all his aspirations cannot leave him in doubt
which he shall choose.

So far as to the effect which the power will produce in
modifying his conception of what is truly desirable.   It
does not make him a hermit, it does not rob him of the
wise man's appreciation of the true worth and use of
money, or power, or position, but it enlightens him, and
teaches him that these things are worthy of his striving
only in so far as they are capable of being assimilated and
employed by the immortal part of his nature, for ends

which stretch far beyond this earth, and are as endless as the eternity towards which he is a wayfarer. But the moment they begin to impede him on his pilgrimage— the moment they become a drag upon his soul, he feels that they are not simply useless, but as necessary to be abandoned as its baggage by a flying army whose only hope of escape lies in speed.

But not merely as influencing the objects of his activity will the power of an endless life display itself. Equally mighty will it be in determining what *principles* are to guide him in gaining what he knows is to be striven for. It is simply the operation in another sphere of the same agency. Nor are we to regard it as a principle working from without. It is not that when a course of action presents itself to him he is obliged to weigh, and ponder, and compare, in order to find out toilsomely whether it is in accordance with certain maxims which have been given him to work by, but which are not in sympathy with his nature. It is rather to be compared—this consciousness of immortality—with the unerring instinct with which the plant selects and absorbs into itself all that it needs from the air and earth around, so as to mount up surely and beautifully in accordance with the type to which it belongs. Put a rose in your garden and it makes no mistake in the elements which it must appropriate—it does not degenerate into a thistle.

So put your heir of immortality into the world, full of the power of an endless life, and he selects with God-given instinct, what his germ of immortality wants; hardly conscious, perhaps, of what he is doing—hardly conscious of all the injurious influences about him striving to poison his soul. The plant is a rose; it cannot change into a thistle.

The man is immortal, and knows it; therefore he can feed only on the food of immortality. Thus, whatever object claims his attention, whether domestic, or social, or political, his instinct rejects all low or earth-born means of gaining it. The gross atmosphere of mere success in attainment stifles him. He must feel,—it is the peremptory law of his existence to feel—that in gaining the temporal and transitory end, he is not compromising truth eternal. He cannot barter the gold of an endless life, for any glittering dross of temporary success. Expediency to him assumes another and a higher meaning than it generally bears. That only is expedient, which is in harmony with the view that makes him no butterfly which shall drop into nothingness when his little day is over, but a child of God, with destinies too mighty to let him entangle himself with low and unworthy motives. He is to live forever, he will not consent to bemire himself. He is to live forever, he cannot stain one day of his eternal existence by forgetting that grand truth.

So too with his more strictly religious life. This is seen to be no separate thing, claiming a little part of his day, to be set aside when he leaves his closet, but an animating principle which leavens his whole existence.

Still, though his entire being be permeated with this thought, there are parts of it on which rests a peculiarly calm and holy light. Even amid the turmoil of activity he can feel that God is near, and He knows that it is best for him to toil. Yet there is a yearning for more immediate intercourse with his Father, which can be satisfied only when these things may be laid aside, and he may surrender himself wholly to communion with his Lord. It is strange that even here, men may forget their immor-

tality. Even when communing with God, the same principle
may assert itself, by force of which men may lose sight of
their heritage of immortality, and one may rest satisfied
with just keeping alive the spark of divine life. But for
him who is indeed under the influence of the principle of
which we speak no such thing is possible. That which is
to live forever must grow, and he cannot grovel on a plane,
but one remove from his who lives as though Heaven were
not. Conscious of the worth of spirituality, he cannot let
anything else overgrow and stifle it. Those will be the
sweet, precious moments of the day, when his soul, communing face to face with Him who is invisible, gathers
fresh strength to resist the lowering influences of earthly
life, and by vanquishing them, converts their noxious
fumes into food, which will nourish the flame of immortal
life within. To him the word of God that speaks to him
of his heritage beyond the grave, will be immeasurably
precious, and the truth which is so dear to him will assert
its natural diffusive power, and impel him to acquaint
those around him with its worth, by preaching the Gospel
as far as in him lies to every creature.

Thus does every department of the Gospel necessarily
imply all the rest. From whatever point you set out, you
find ere long that every one of God's truths must embrace
all the others as it is developed, and the power of an endless life once fairly implanted stretches its influence over
the whole man.

These things of which I have been speaking, my friends,
are no mystical and impracticable speculations. The state
which I have described is not only possible for you to
reach, but will be your sin if you do not.

The power of an endless life is the property of every

Christian. Nothing but a melancholy declension in faith and zeal, can permit you to ignore this fact. As you are even dimly aware of the high destiny which belongs to you as an immortal being, I charge you to remember this, and to strive that it be an ever-present thought, that you are disgracing your soul, despising God, trampling under foot His blessed Son, just in proportion as this truth drops out of your horizon, and you contentedly grovel on a lower plane than befits the child of the King eternal, immortal, and invisible.

XVII.

CERTAINTY.

"If we love one another, God dwelleth in us, and His love is perfected in us. Hereby know we that we dwell in Him and He in us because He hath given us of His Spirit."—1 St. John iv. 12, 13.

ONE of the latest acquirements of the Christian soul is the perpetual maintenance of that certainty of which St. John here speaks. It does not seem indeed, as though God designed us to have it in just the way in which we have it regarding many matters of our daily life.

If this be so—if, on the one hand, the certainty attainable here is of a different kind from that of common experience, and if, on the other, its *evidence* is of a different sort, it may well be that mistaken hopes and expectations stand in the way of gaining even that which is put within our reach: we may be anxiously looking out for the appearance of something unlike what we shall ever see, and looking too in the wrong direction. That we do crave sure knowledge about our present condition and our spiritual destinies is undeniable, at least where any intensity of Christian feeling exists. That most of us have from time to time, in this department of being, a dim, shadowy presentiment, I think very probable. Nor is such a feeling of the impossibility of forecasting the future at all an unmingled evil. If we were beyond the reach of temptation—if our earthly probation were over, and we had entered on the enjoyment of Paradise—then such a lack of absolute certainty would constitute a sinful doubt of the

206

unconditional promise of God. But the awful possibilities of our sinful nature are so often disclosed to us by the unlooked-for manifestations that evil tendencies which we thought killed are still alive—the passions that seemed well gotten under, raise their hateful heads again so defiantly—the lusts of the flesh, or the murderous instincts are so plainly not altogether quelled—that any such certainty as would absolutely put us at rest, and enable us to think no more about our final destiny would be pernicious to the last degree. All this is evident. And the craving for such a kind of certainty has been felt in every age. For a long period it found satisfaction and excuse in the doctrine of Predestination and Election. The references made in Scripture to God's plans and His foreknowledge, in this matter of men's eternal salvation, were eagerly laid hold of, systematized, and promulgated with strange disregard to the plain way in which salvation is spoken of as open to all; and in its later form of Calvinism, as embraced by the sternest, sturdiest, gloomiest races of Europe, it had an influence over the human mind, and the tenor of common life, which we can but dimly conceive. Of course, and by the confession of all saner minds, it was utterly impossible for any man to arrive at certainty on the most important point of all, namely whether he, himself were among the number predestinated to eternal bliss. But this does not seem to have seriously hindered the sway of the doctrine in Scotland, in New England, or among Cromwell's Roundheads. And, maligned as it has been from Hudibras down to Theodore Parker, or Froude, its general effect for a long period was not inconsistent with a condition of private morals and public purity of motive, hardly to be matched by any contemporary system.

These tenets may now to a very large extent, be said to have lost their vitality, or at least their prominence. Most men who think upon the subject feel that God must at least have foreknown the destiny of each soul that was to be brought into the world; and so it may be, as our seventeenth Article nobly phrases it, that "Godly consideration of Predestination, and our Election in Christ, is full of sweet, pleasant, and unspeakable comfort to godly persons, and such as feel in themselves the working of the Spirit of Christ, mortifying the works of the flesh, and their earthly members, and drawing up their minds to high and heavenly things." But this is only as a part of their common Christian life, and not at all as furnishing that absolute and unconditional certainty to which it once so largely gave birth. Where it once begot a hard, self-satisfied assurance among those who seemed least entitled to it, the same class of men now-a-days have come to cheer themselves with an easy confidence quite as harmful, and much less logical. But with neither of these attitudes of mind do I now propose to deal. I wish to speak rather upon a point of high importance for those whose religious lives are real, and deep, and reverent, but who have never made clear to themselves just how, or how far, they may and should be confident in regard to the genuineness and hopefulness of their experience. To many, no doubt, this class will seem both too small in number, and too weak in character, to deserve much attention. In both respects such an estimate would be wrong. Even where this is not the habitual mood, most of us have occasional experience of it; and every minister's intercourse with his people, in ordinary life, and still more as death draws near, reveals to him the existence of this state of mind among those whom he has come to love and reverence. And if any class has a claim upon our sympathy more than another, it is surely the quiet, uncomplaining company of the world's unseen martyrs, who cannot take it as a place of happiness, but bear their cross with silent steps and downcast head along the byways of earth. Such characters as these in the master-pieces of literature, win from the reader his readiest, deepest, reverence. And those to whom experience reveals them in actual life, are not *less* ready certainly with their sympathy and respect.

A certainty like that of the multiplication-table is not to be expected in regard to our eternal destiny : but as to our being the children of God, here spoken of as dwelling in Him, and having Him to dwell in us, of this, St. John assures us we may be certain. Let us look at some of our uncertainties and their causes.

With modest, humble, souls the most common subject of doubt is the reality of their own spiritual lives—the genuineness of their love to God. At times, they have no doubt. At times, the man is so full of devotion and thankfulness, Christ seems personally so near, that even the sorest burdens of life are borne with ease, and more than submission. And by the burdens he is thus enabled to bear, I do not mean those alone which concern him individually, and those near to him, but rather the sight of the weary, blind, sinful world about him, that goes on so recklessly spending its swiftly-fleeting time for winning eternal life, so little recking of the things that are for its deepest bliss. Even this he can bear; not in the sense of shutting his eyes to it, and forgetting it—not by thinking that, after all, wrong may be nearer akin to right, sin to holiness— but by the inflow of a deeper faith, that helps him to know with happy assurance, that through it all God is working out a plan such as becomes His infinite wisdom and His tender, all-embracing love.

But then there are other moods in which to-day's weakness, or actual sin, sets him thinking whether such unworthy returns for God's mercy could be if he were really His child. That impatient word, could it have come from one whose body is indeed the temple of the Holy Ghost? That vile thought that thrust itself into the mind, and which he suffered to linger there for a time with pleasure, if he were truly a new man, dead unto sin and alive unto righteousness, would not its known sinfulness have caused it at once to be rejected with loathing? The dulness and feebleness—the almost lack of desire for their being granted —with which this morning's prayers were uttered, how could such things be in a soul indeed regenerated? And all these have the other side: they must bear equally sad testimony to God's not having so truly adopted him—not taking that fatherly oversight of his welfare which at other times seems so clear. How is he to strike the balance between these two alternating states? In his brightest, freest moments of rejoicing, there is much more of sinfulness present, than there is of holiness in the other sinful mood. Does not this mean, after all, that holiness has not even the upper hand? still less is supreme ruler?

I go into these details because they occur so often, and because I always feel myself more satisfied when I have reason to think that my spiritual physician knows what is the matter with me. When one recognizes in Robertson's sermons the graphic picture of one's own experience of weariness and misgiving, one feels the better able to draw from his brave words the cheer for which, in such moods one thirsts, and the inimitable charm of language is not alone what renders those few volumes of discourses so lastingly dear to men's hearts. It is because of another quality, I think, that we love them so : because they create in us the feeling that the words are not mere words, but the outcome of personal knowledge. He has created, almost, a new style in these matters, and he who would speak helpfully to men must try at least to make them see that, whatever his deficiencies otherwise, he does not lack the sympathy that springs from a common experience.

For those then who are familiar with this lack of certainty, and who so long for it, the grave question is ever coming back : How may I gain the assurance of which St. John here speaks so unhesitatingly? Knowing as I do, that there are states of mind in which holiness is less winning than the passing gratification that I know to be wrong, is it not gross presumption to trust that these holier aspirations are trustworthy signs of my being the child of God? The evidence on which St. John here rests —the possession of the Spirit—is one that needs amplification before the fulness of its answer is apparent. Let us go back a little further and see *why* he lays such stress upon it.

Which is the natural tendency, of these two of which you are conscious? Which is the one you were born with—the one which is most akin to the spirit that characterizes mankind so far as it is left to itself? Books and thoughts belonging to the purely worldly sphere, which side of your nature do they appeal to? There can be no question here. The natural state—that which would be your permanent condition, if you simply allowed things to take their own course within, and made no conscientious effort—this state is the original one. It may and will grow worse—it may and will be accompanied by remonstrance, more or less feeble from the higher part of your nature; but it is that in which you were born,—it is sinful, and left to yourself, you would have continued wholly in it. It might not have burst out into crime, or overt wickedness of any kind; but the distinctive mark of it is that holiness is not its aim, nor the presence of a holy God the place in which it delights. Now with this part of your nature you are familiar enough—only too painfully familiar with it, and it is *its* persistent opposition to improvement that makes you often doubt as to your being indeed a child of God.

But if, as has been already said so often, this be the natural state, what are you to say about this other disposition that maintains such a struggle against it? Weak as it often is, it never yields to worse impulses without your knowing that if you had chosen to exert your power, the victory would have been on the other side. You feel that on the whole it is gaining on the other and original disposition towards wrong. Here is a most remarkable set of facts. An inclination toward what we may at least call non-holiness was born with you—forms part of human nature as it has displayed itself through history for thousands of years. You find it strong within you. And yet here is another disposition, fighting against it continually, and slowly gaining ground upon it. Whence came this latter? Can it, in the sense of being a real potent factor in your life, be natural too? Your inmost consciousness denies this, and instinctively attributes to it a higher, nay a divine origin. God hath given you His Spirit.

If I were speaking for the purpose of logically convincing

gainsayers, another course would perhaps be preferable. But I am addressing myself to men and women who share with me the knowledge of these internal facts, and between whom and me there is only the question how to arrange them, and to which set of facts the greater importance should be given. And to them I am trying to show that where a higher, holier state is replacing, or to any considerable degree has replaced, the natural, sinful one, there they have a *right* to that triumphant conviction of which St. John speaks, because the wrong would not be conquered by the right unless the right were stronger; or as the same Apostle phrases it "Greater is He that is in us, than he that is in the world. Hereby know we that we dwell in Him and He in us, because He hath given us of His Spirit." Rightly viewed, the question as to the genuineness of your soul's life is not one as to whether you have become holy enough to satisfy yourself, but whether you are growing holier at all, or indeed, not even so much as that, because that is a test at times very hard to apply. It is just this: do you know and feel that you are *in earnest* to become holy. If you know *that*, you have the assurance of which St. John here speaks. If you know that, the genuineness of your religious life is sufficiently proved; and seriously to doubt that God is working in you is sinful disbelief of the best evidence He could give you.

But we may go further and find valuable truth in the words here chosen, to convey to the faithful heart a much-needed lesson. *His* Spirit which He hath *given* us.

The Christian who longs to see, and where he cannot see, at least to believe, that in the men about him there is more good than appears on the surface, often brings confusion into his own ways of regarding things by making this

effort amiss. Let me explain myself. You look out into
the world around you, and see many men who exert themselves nobly and vigorously for the good of their fellow-
creatures. With the pen, by laborious, patient thought,
by devising new social schemes that may make the good
things of life more accessible to all, and raise the tone of
thinking and acting,—in all these fields of activity work
is done more and more largely as the world grows older.
You are glad of it; you rejoice over it, not only with the
joy of feeling that after-generations will find the world a
brighter place than their forefathers have done, but also
for the conviction that the higher the aims which men have,
and the greater the opportunities furnished them, the
arger the likelihood that they will be Christians. You
use that word in your thoughts and anticipations because
to you it means most in the way of happiness and goodness. All such feelings are right, are natural to him who
in the love of God for men sees a larger ground for hope.
And to the men too, who are thus laboring to better the
world's condition, you must reach out a cordial hand so
far as their self-sacrifice extends. But when you find that
they distinctly disavow any religious motive or object —
when, as in the case of a certain school in England, or on
the continent, the thought of God, or of conscience, or of
a future life is rejected and scoffed at—when the schemes
for reconstructing society aim at abolishing all that is best
and fairest now, from the family down, it is in but a very
modified sense that you believe the Spirit of God to be
working among them. How shall you regard such? This
is a question full of difficulty to the Christian thinker.
Without the grossest lack of charity he cannot deny them
great sincerity in their endeavors. But if he is to recognize

here any further influence of God than using these men as instruments for the furtherance of his ends, he feels that he must give up all that has grown clear to him as to God's working. He stands face to face with this alternative: shall I abandon all that my deepest experience has proved to me; or shall I deny that the spirit which leads to such results as these is God's Spirit? The denial may be made with all charity; but one of these two courses must, I think, be taken. And the harm that comes from trying to follow neither to the full is what has led me to speak of it in this connection. If you take a position mid-way between the two, you so confuse your religious beliefs and princi-ples, that the state of doubt as to your own position be-comes, of necessity, almost habitual. Unless (for your own private use) you define one of these spirits to be, and the other not to be, the Spirit of God, everything between these two extremes may slowly become laudable and proper. You may think I am raising a very unsubstantial spectre; and in some minds, no doubt, the danger is less here than elsewhere. But I am greatly mistaken if those who have carefully watched the effect of these modern influences on the minds of the younger generation of read-ing men, will not agree that a loosely held religious belief is very often destroyed in just this way. Where the essen-tially supernatural character of religion is not maintained, it has little power of resistance. And therefore I would urge the importance of this phrase of St. John—urge the necessity in all our thinking and doing, of regarding our religious life as being the work of *God's* Spirit which He hath *given* us.

I am fully alive to the charge that may be brought against the advice I have given, as being peculiarly full of what Harriet Martineau calls the disgusting selfishness of Christians. To urge men, for their own peace of mind, to set down other laborers for human good, as inspired by a low spirit,—this caricature of my advice is certainly loathsome enough. But after all, which is best?—to have definite views to live by, or to find a new Gospel every day? And I would urge definiteness, not only on the ground that without it our highest aims as Christians are terribly jeoparded, but especially for the good of others —from the deepest, tenderest regard for them. If in any degree we believe the spirit of Christianity to be the highest manifestation of the Spirit of God, the duty flows inevitably from this of maintaining it in word and deed. What would you think of the teacher of a school who taught that the sun moves round the earth, or who left it an open question? What of a teacher of moral philosophy who left undecided the propriety of lying and stealing? And every one of us is a teacher, whose instructions, as I am impelled again and again to repeat, are heeded. You are doing your fellow-men the highest good when you impress upon them most distinctly the truth that there is a God, and that the Christ of the New Testament and of the Church is His Son. Amidst the jarring systems of opinion that have their day and cease to be (not however, without profoundly influencing a generation for good or for evil), Christianity still rears its august form. Its authority has been vastly weakened by internal divisions; but hitherto those divisions have not been about denials of absolutely essential truth. Those who most love their race, and would most readily work for its good, are they who contemplate with deepest anxiety the threatened approach of the day, when its adherents shall deliberately forego the power, and lose the desire, to distinguish between the Spirit of God and the spirit of Belial.

And that, not from selfishness, but from love for men. If we love one another, God dwelleth in us, and His love is perfected in us. The love that Christ bore to His followers, He, Himself proposes, as the model for our love toward one another. The life of the individual believer, like that of the Church on earth, is full of changes and chances such as befall every thing here and now. But I have tried to tell you how God gives us richly to enjoy the certainty that He dwells within us. These very conflicts that so disturb us are the proof; for the lessening power of evil which still struggles against good within us is manifestly due to the Spirit which helpeth our infirmities, —can be due to nothing else But we shall work along with Him best as we learn more exactly what are the good works He hath prepared for us to walk in; as we hold fast by the truth He teaches us evermore firmly and clearly. And our work as promulgators and heralds of His truth will likewise be fruitful in direct proportion as we remember the solemn responsibility of accepting and spreading nothing but what our deepest experience confirms as true; as agreeable to the wholesome words of our Lord Jesus Christ, and the doctrine which is according to godliness.

Such is the truest love to God and man, and the brave, manly, reverential mood in which we deal the hardest blows at sin and falsehood without and within, because we glory in our God and in the calling wherewith He hath called us. Of such a spiritual warrior in his conflicts it is said, as of Sir Galahad in his earthly combat,

10

His good blade carves the casques of men,
　His tough lance thrusteth sure,
His strength is as the strength of ten,
　Because his heart is pure.
So keeps he fair through faith and prayer,
　A virgin heart in work and will.

Lightning Source UK Ltd.
Milton Keynes UK
19 January 2011

165974UK00006BA/71/P

9 781149 544297